The Autho

Pamela Brooks, who lives in Norwich children, is a prolific author with many successful books to her name. She also works on a freelance basis as a copy editor, copywriter and journalist. Educated at Wymondham College, she went on to read English at the University of Leicester.

Norwich: Stories of a City

PAMELA BROOKS

FORT PUBLISHING LTD

First published in 2003 by Fort Publishing Ltd, Old Belmont
House, 12 Robsland Avenue, Ayr, KA7 2RW (01292-880693).

Printed by Bell and Bain Ltd, Glasgow.

Typeset by S. Fairgrieve (0131-658-1763).

ISBN 0-9544461-0-0

For Gerard, Chris and Chloë
with all my love

CONTENTS

PREFACE

Norwich is more than just the most easterly city in the British Isles (one degree eighteen minutes, if we're being precise). It's a place where we 'do different'. At one point it was the third largest city in England. It had two pubs for every day of the year and a church for every week – and still has more medieval churches than any other city in western Europe. Our city walls enclose a larger area than any other city walls in England – including London – and our cathedral has the second-tallest spire in England (second only to Salisbury) and the largest cloisters in Europe. We have the second most important civic regalia in the country, and our guildhall is second in size only to London's. Norwich originally had a mint, and also became a temporary mint in the seventeenth century; in the recoinage of 1695, £259,000 worth of half-crowns, shillings and sixpences (all bearing the letter N) were minted in a corner of the cloisters in St Andrew's Hall.

In terms of communications, Norwich has notched up its share of firsts. The first provincial newspaper in Britain was published here (the *Norwich Post* in 1701), and the first book written in English by a woman was written in the city (*Revelations of Divine Love* by Julian of Norwich in 1395). The first commercial long-distance telephone-call in the country was made on 1 November 1878, between Cannon Street in London and Colman's accounting office in Norwich, and the postal-code system was first developed and tested here.

In terms of culture, too, Norwich has come first. The first free library in Britain was established in 1857. And England's first-ever non-denominational cemetery was founded here in 1821; Thomas Drummond intended that anyone could be buried at the Rosary Cemetery with the services of the creed and minister of their choice, and some great philanthropists were buried there, including A. J. Caley and J. J. Colman.

So it's unsurprising that Norwich has many, many tales to tell. I've only scratched the surface here but I hope I'll inspire you to find out more about the 'fine city' George Borrow dubbed us.

I would like to thank the following people who've given generously of their time in the making of this book – in alphabetical order: Stewart Alexander (Castle Museum); Derek Briggs (Castle Museum); Paul Durrant (Archant); Mike King (Assembly House); Roger King (Caley's); Phil Lovett; Lesley Owen-Edwards (Unilever); Tim Pestell (Castle Museum); Hilary Shanks (Start-rite); Marilyn Taylor (Castle Museum). Not forgetting the endless patience of the staff of the Millennium Library's local-history section!

Pamela Brooks
Norwich, April 2003

1

'I AM GLAD TO DIE FOR MY COUNTRY'

Edith Louisa Cavell was born on 4 December 1865 at Swardeston Vicarage, just outside Norwich, the eldest of four children. She was educated at home by her father, Revd Frederick Cavell, and he taught her three important principles which lasted her whole life and contributed to her death: thought for others, self-sacrifice and prayer.

Edith was determined and strong-willed at an early age. When her father needed a room for his Sunday school, she wrote to the Bishop of Norwich to ask for his help. The bishop agreed to help on condition that the village raised some of the cash. Edith and her sister painted cards and sold them, helping to raise £300 for the church room, then wrote to the bishop again and reminded him of his promise. The room was duly built next to the vicarage.

As a teenager, Edith was educated at Norwich High School before attending boarding schools in Kensington and Bristol. She then went to Laurel Court in Peterborough, where she trained to become a teacher. She was so good at French that the school principal, Margaret Gibson, recommended her to the Francois family in Brussels as governess to their children.

When Edith's father became ill in 1895, she returned home to look after him and decided that she wanted to become a nurse. She entered the London Hospital Nurses' Training School in 1896, and was one of six nurses seconded to help with the typhoid epidemic in Maidstone. It turned out that only 132 of the 1,700 people who caught it died, and Edith received the Maidstone Medal for her work. Her boss, Eva Lückes, criticised her, saying that she was unpunctual, wasn't 'very much in earnest', couldn't 'altogether be depended on' and would have been a better nurse if she had put her whole heart into it. However, Miss Lückes almost never gave good reports!

Edith became a night supervisor at the St Pancras Infirmary in 1899 – soul-destroying work, as it was a Poor Law institution and around 25 per cent of the paupers there died of chronic illness. She moved to Shoreditch as assistant matron three years later and pioneered follow-up visits by going to see patients after she'd discharged them. She then moved to Manchester, filling in as matron for the Queen's District Nursing Home.

In 1906, the Belgian surgeon Antoine Depage wanted to establish a hospital outside the boundaries of the religious orders which controlled the nursing in his country. He needed a matron with administrative experience who could speak French, and the Francois family recommended Edith. The training school opened in October 1907 and Edith loved her new role. She was so enthusiastic that the Berkendael Institute in Brussels became one of the largest sources of trained nurses for hospitals and nursing homes. By 1912 she was providing nurses for three hospitals, twenty-four communal schools and thirteen kindergartens, and by 1914 she was giving four lectures a week to nurses and doctors. In one of her last letters, Edith wrote of the joy she'd felt at being called to organise the first school of graduate nurses in Belgium.

She was also a strict taskmaster, despite what Miss Lückes thought about Edith's own lack of punctuality. Under Edith's supervision any nurse more than two minutes late for breakfast would forfeit two hours of her own time! Though in one of her last letters, Edith asked some of her students to forgive what they may have seen as her severity, as she loved them more than they knew.

In 1914, Edith was on holiday in Norwich, visiting her mother, when she heard about the outbreak of war. She went straight back to Brussels, saying she would be 'needed more than ever' at a time like this. Although Belgium was initially a neutral country at the start of the war, it was occupied by the Germans from 1914, apart from a small amount of territory around La Panne, Furnes and Ypres which was held by the Allied forces. Albert I, the King of Belgium, set up his headquarters at La Panne and stayed there with his troops throughout the war.

In September 1914, the engineer Herman Capaiu arrived at the hospital and told Edith about the Allied soldiers who had become separated from their units and trapped behind enemy lines. Edith immediately offered her help – despite knowing that the Germans would shoot any Allied soldiers they found, as well as the people hiding them – and took in Lieutenant-Colonel Dudley Boger and Sergeant Fred Meachin of the 1st Battalion of the Cheshire Regiment. She sheltered them for two weeks and then arranged for someone to take them to neutral territory in Holland.

Herman Capaiu reported her help to the Prince and Princess de Croy, who headed a resistance group at Mons. Princess Maria de Croy had established a Red Cross hospital in her chateau at the beginning of the war and was so upset when thirteen British soldiers were tracked down to a haystack and shot near the chateau that she decided to organise a system to help soldiers in hiding and send them to Brussels. Philippe Baucq, an architect in Brussels, was responsible for providing people who would take the soldiers to Holland. Edith Cavell was recruited into their organisation.

Edith undertook most of the rescue work at the hospital herself, not wanting to put her nurses in danger; she'd even sewn her diary into a cushion so that no one else could be incriminated. At one time, according to Louise Thuliez who worked in the same group, Edith was hiding thirty-five escapees, including a Belgian collaborator. She rescued some soldiers from her native Norfolk, among them Arthur Wood from the 1st Battalion of the Norfolk Regiment, and asked him to take home her Bible and a letter to her mother.

When the Germans initially entered Brussels on 20 August 1914, they'd allowed Edith to remain as matron of the institute and converted her training school into a Red Cross institute. Although Edith was officially of enemy nationality, her Red Cross status protected her. But, by 1915, the Germans suspected that someone was helping Allied soldiers to escape, and they'd heard rumours about Edith. They placed the hospital under observation. Tragedy also struck the hospital when Madame Depage – Antoine's wife and a personal friend of Edith – was drowned after the *Lusitania* was sunk by German forces.

On 31 July 1915, the Germans arrested Philippe Baucq and

another operative from the escape-route team. On 5 August Otto Mayer of the German secret police arrested Edith. They questioned her for seventy-two hours; when she told them nothing, they told her they knew everything and if she made a full confession it would save her friends. She believed them, and confessed.

Brand Whitlock, the minister at the American Legation in Belgium during the war, heard that Edith had been arrested. Whitlock had previously obtained agreement from the German regime that they would tell him when any American citizen was arrested, or anyone else whose interests he was looking after, so that he could help defend them in court. Edith was British and therefore he felt that he was looking after her interests, so he wrote to Baron von der Lancken, the German minister in Brussels, asking if it was true that Edith Cavell had been arrested. He also asked if *Maitre* de Leval, the Belgian legal adviser to the American Legation, could see Edith and help to prepare her defence. Von der Lancken wrote back to say that Edith was in solitary confinement in the prison of St Gilles and had admitted to hiding English and French soldiers in her home, giving them money to get to France and providing guides to help them cross the Dutch frontier. He also said that her defence was in the hands of *Maitre* Thomas Braun and he couldn't permit de Leval to visit.

Shortly before the trial, Braun told Whitlock that the Germans had forbidden him to plead before the military court, and he suggested using the lawyer *Maitre* Sadi Kirschen. On Thursday 7 October 1915, Edith's case came before the German court-martial. The trial was held in the Senate chamber of the National Palace and the rich carpets, gilt frescoes and plush red chairs were in stark contrast to the military guards packed into the room. Edith was brought before the court with the Princess de Croy, the Countess de Belleville and thirty-two others. Their own counsel and the witnesses were seated behind them so that the accused were unable either to see or communicate with them.

The charge brought against her was 'having conspired to violate the German Military Penal Code' and 'conducting troops to the enemy', which equated to treason and was punishable by the death penalty, though no written statement of her crime had been given to Edith or her lawyer. In any event she hadn't actually conducted troops to the enemy. She'd *sheltered* them. Whitlock described Edith as 'a frail and delicate little woman about 40 years of age . . . with a conscience almost Puritan, and was very stern with herself in what she conceived to be her duty'.

The trial lasted for two days. Her friends all expected her to be sent to a German prison with a sentence of anything between two and twenty years, and that she would be freed when peace was concluded. The interrogation took place in German, which Edith didn't speak, so the questions and responses were translated into French. And nobody could verify that the translations were accurate.

When the court asked if she'd helped English soldiers left behind after the battles of Mons and Charleroi, she said yes; they were English and she was English, and she would help her own. When they asked her if she'd helped twenty, she replied: 'More than twenty – two hundred.' She then admitted that they weren't all English; they were French and Belgian, too. One of the judges said she was foolish to help English soldiers because they were ungrateful. Edith protested that wasn't true, because 'some of them have written from England to thank me'.

That protest sealed her fate. She was found guilty and sentenced to death by firing squad.

The ambassadors of the United States and Spain both tried to intercede but got nowhere. At 9 p.m. on the Monday evening, de Leval told Whitlock that the death sentence had been pronounced at 4.30 that afternoon and Edith was to be shot the next day. Whitlock signed a *recours en grace*, a plea for mercy, and de Leval went to find Baron von der Lancken. The Baron took some persuading to speak on behalf of the woman he called 'that spy' (even though she hadn't actually been charged with spying, just helping soldiers to leave Belgium) but eventually agreed to speak to the military governor, General von Saubersweig. However, von Saubersweig refused to change his mind about the execution or even to receive the plea for mercy.

Pastor Le Seur was a German chaplain appointed to minister to the prisoners. He asked Edith if he could help and she asked him to inform her 80-year-old mother so that she wouldn't learn of her death in the newspapers. Le Seur was a Lutheran and realised that Edith couldn't receive the holy sacrament from someone outside the Anglican church, so he asked her if she could accept it from Revd Stirling Gahan, the Anglican chaplain in Brussels.

Le Seur obtained a permit for Gahan to visit Edith and, when he arrived, she was lying on the cot in her cell. She rose and put on a dressing gown, then told him she wasn't afraid to die and that she'd written to her mother and friends. She also sent a message to one of her nurses, who had developed a morphine habit, telling her to be brave and that if God would permit Edith would continue to try to help her. She read and reflected during those weeks and gained much solace from her Bible, prayer book and Thomas à Kempis's book *The Imitation of Christ*. She insisted that she had no hatred and no regrets and received the holy sacrament. Her last words to Gahan were, 'I am thankful to have had these ten weeks of quiet to get ready. Now I have had them and have been kindly treated here. I expected my sentence and I believe it was just. Standing as I do in view of God and Eternity, I realise that patriotism is not enough. I must have no hatred and no bitterness towards anyone.'

Edith had been told that she would be called at 5 a.m. Le Seur had offered to accompany her from the prison rather than meet her at the Tir Nationale (the National Rifle Range). He described her cell as being like 'a vault' with 'two large bouquets of withered flowers'. Edith had packed all her property into her handbag. They passed in silence through the long corridors and at 6 a.m. a motor car took her and Philippe Baucq to the Tir Nationale. They were met by 250 soldiers and placed in front of two firing squads of eight men.

The sentence was read aloud. Le Seur was permitted a last word with Edith, who said to him, 'Ask Mr Gahan to tell my loved ones later on that my soul, as I believe, is safe, and that I am glad to die for my country.' Le Seur led her to the execution post; she was loosely bound to it and a bandage placed round her eyes. At the command, the firing squad – standing six paces away – shot Edith and Baucq. Le Seur was shocked to see reflex movements with Edith raising herself up silently three times, her hands stretched upwards. One shot had gone through her forehead, making her face stream with blood, and there were bullet holes 'as large as a fist' in her back. Her coffin was lowered into the grave and Le Seur prayed over it, then 'went home, almost sick in my soul'.

Edith Cavell didn't want to be remembered as a martyr or a heroine but simply as 'a nurse who tried to do her duty'. However, when news of her death was announced, it swayed neutral opinion against Germany and recruitment in Britain doubled for eight weeks. That morning, after the execution, Whitlock asked if the American Legation and Edith's friends could bury her, but Baron von Lancken replied that the body had already been interred and couldn't be exhumed without an order from the Imperial Government.

After the end of World War I, Edith's body was exhumed, and the post mortem confirmed that three bullets had pierced her heart. Her body was returned to home soil. On 15 May 1919, King George V led a memorial service at Westminster Abbey, which was also attended by Queen Alexandra, Princess Victoria and nursing representatives from around the world. Then her body was taken to Norwich by special train. Following the procession to the cathedral, Bishop Pollock described her as 'alive in God' and as someone who taught us that our patriotism must be examined in the light of something higher. Edith was reburied on Life's Green at Norwich Cathedral. Her name lives on in the city: in the memorial on Tombland, just outside the Cathedral walls; in the Edith Cavell pub, almost opposite; and in Cavell Road, just off the outer ring road.

2

OLD CROME

John Crome was unusual among painters in that he actually stayed in the place where he was born. Norwich was his birthplace, the place where he worked, the subject of his paintings and also his market. Of the 307 pictures he exhibited, only 16 were shown in London. He also etched thirty-three plates (which he didn't publish) and founded Britain's first provincial art society. And although he became known as one of the three major landscape artists of the age (with Turner and Constable), he wrote with difficulty, visited Paris and Wales once during his lifetime (he paid his way on the Welsh trip by painting signs for the inns where he stayed), and had a yearly visit to London. Other than that, he stayed put.

His most famous paintings include: *Mousehold Heath, near Norwich* (now in the National Gallery); *Clump of Trees, Hautbois Common*; *Oak at Poringland*; *Willow*; *Coast Scene near Yarmouth*; *Bruges, on the Ostend River*; *Slate Quarries*; *Italian Boulevards*; *Fishmarket at Boulogne*.

He had quite an impact on the city of his birth. George Borrow wrote about him in *Lavengro* and Dawson Turner (who was a partner in Gurney's Yarmouth Bank, the boss of Crome's son Fred, and wrote a memoir of Crome) described him as 'frank, honourable and disinterested in disposition, lively and instructive in conversation, and possessing a cheerful and social temper, united to a most winning naivete of manners – excellent also in his moral character, as a husband, a father and a friend.'

John Crome was born on Friday 23 December 1768, the son of a journeyman weaver who kept the Griffin Tavern in Conisford Street, which is now King Street, the part that was on the edge of

Castle Meadow (a painting of the Griffin by D. Hodgson shows a two-storey house with steep gables and a thatched roof, opposite Griffin Lane). He was baptised on Christmas Day in St George's church, Colegate. Not much is known of his early life but, in 1781, Crome became an errand boy at the apothecary's shop and surgery of Dr Edward Rigby in Pitt Lane, which led from Willow Lane across St Giles to Bethel Street. Crome lived over the surgery in a second-floor garret.

Crome clearly had a sense of mischief, as legend has it that he sometimes changed the labels on medicines he was supposed to deliver. He once bled a patient in Rigby's absence, allegedly almost to the point of death. But then some of Rigby's students played a trick on him, putting the skeleton they used for anatomical instruction in Crome's bed with the aim of scaring him. It didn't scare him in the slightest, but he was annoyed enough to throw the skeleton out of the window and it smashed on the flagstones of the court below. So it was time for the errand boy to move on.

In 1783, Crome became apprentice to the coach painter and signwriter Francis Whisler, at 55 Bethel Street, next to the Coach and Horses Inn. His indenture was on 1 August 1783, to be apprenticed to Whisler for seven years, bound by his father John Crome the victualler and witnessed by Robert Batey and Thomas Barker, Jr. According to the terms of his apprenticeship, Crome was obliged to serve his master, keep his secrets and 'his lawful commands everywhere gladly do'. He was neither allowed to waste or to lend his master's goods, nor to buy or sell without his master's consent. He wasn't allowed to get married (or commit fornication), go to inns, taverns and alehouses, or play cards or dice 'or any other unlawful games'. Crome signed 'of his own free will' and with his father's consent. On Whisler's side, the contract was to teach Crome how to be a 'House and Coach Painter', give him enough food and accommodation, 'good and sufficient' clothes and shoes (plus 'washing and mending of same during said term'), and Crome's father had to 'find proper physic and nurses' if Crome fell ill.

During his apprenticeship, Crome learned how to grind and

mix paints and in addition painted signs for several Norwich inns, including the Sawyers and the Two Brewers. However, the nineteenth-century curator James Reeve, who assembled most of the documentary evidence about Crome, said it was 'nonsense' that Crome learned to engrave while under Whisler's tuition.

In this period, Crome also became friendly with Bob Ladbrooke, an apprentice to the printer and engraver White in London Lane. The story goes that Crome and Ladbrooke hired a garret so they could paint small landscapes and portraits, which they then sold. Though during his lifetime, Crome didn't make huge sums from his art. In fact the most that any of his paintings fetched was around £50, and he often gave people paintings in lieu of payment.

By 1790, Crome had made his first sketch in oils. He'd also been introduced to Thomas Harvey of Catton – possibly by Dr Rigby – who became one of his patrons. Harvey owned a landscape picture by the Dutch master Meindert Hobbema, which is said to have inspired Crome. At Harvey's house, Crome also met Sir William Beechey, who said: 'Crome, when I first knew him, was an awkward, unformed country lad, but shrewd in all his remarks on art.'

Crome married Phoebe Berney in October 1792; at the end of the month, their first child Abigail was born, though she died less than two years later. They lived in a terrace just off St George's Street in Green Lane. The houses there were pulled down and replaced by 'Layers Terrace' in 1901, which was in turn demolished in the 1962 slum clearance to make way for part of the inner ring road. A stone plaque from the terraces, which has a medallion plaque of Crome, is kept in the Bridewell museum. It reads: 'Old Crome, 1768–1821, Founder of the Norwich School of Painters, lived in a house on this site'.

Crome fell ill in 1793; he was admitted to Norwich hospital with hydrocele (an abnormal collection of fluid in the membranes surrounding the testes) in March and remained there for two months. He was readmitted in September for another two months with the same complaint. Though his illness didn't appear adversely to affect his marriage, because he and Phoebe were blessed with five sons and two daughters between 1793 and 1813. They included John Berney Crome, born in 1794, who was also a gifted painter (and the reason why Crome was known as 'Old Crome', to distinguish between the two), and Emily Crome, who painted flower pieces. Crome's dying advice to the younger Crome was apparently, 'John, me boy, paint, but paint for fame; and if your subject is a pigsty – dignify it!'

Crome also became a drawing teacher. His pupils included the son of the Quaker wine merchant William Sparshall (for a fee of 1 guinea for the half-year plus 18s 9d for pencils, chalk, sheet paper and rubber). He was appointed as the drawing master to the Gurney family, on the recommendation of Thomas Harvey and Edward Rigby. In 1798 an entry in Richenda Gurney's journal refers to Crome and how vexing her sister, 'Betsey' Gurney (later the prison reformer Elizabeth Fry), was. Richenda was annoyed because Crome paid more attention to Betsey than to her! Crome was also briefly the drawing teacher to Dawson Turner's daughters. He was still painting signs. A bill in the British Museum for £2 4s dates from May 1803, and relates to his fee for painting the sign of the Lame Dog, writing and gilding the board for the Lamb and writing and gilding the name on the Maid's Head.

On 19 February 1803 the Norwich Society was formed. Its purpose was 'An Enquiry into the Rise, Progress and present state of Painting, Architecture and Sculpture, with a view to point out the Best Methods of study to attain to Greater Perfection in these Arts.' Gurney, Dr Rigby (who was then mayor) and Harvey were patrons, and Crome was one of the founder members. The society held fortnightly meetings at the Hole in the Wall tavern (which occupied the former site of St Crucis's church) on Exchange Street. The meetings entailed supper and the reading of papers; there was a yearly subscription of four guineas.

The society grew, and moved to Wrench's Court, which was located behind Sir Benjamin Wrench's house in Pottergate. The house later became the New Lobster Inn and once sported a sign saying 'the North Pole is in a direct line from this spot'. In the first exhibition, held in August 1805, there were 223 works. Of these, Crome had twenty-two exhibits; some were sketches and some watercolours, including a view of Carrow Abbey. His friend Bob Ladbrooke was also a member of the society, and was already an exhibitor in the Royal Academy.

In 1806 Crome exhibited two landscapes at the Royal Academy. It's believed that he attended himself because his name was shown as 'Croom' (his pronunciation) in the index and against one picture, whereas it was spelled 'Crome' against the other picture. The same year, the landscape painter John Sell Cotman joined the Norwich Society and, in the following year, Crome was elected president.

In 1811, Crome went to Derbyshire. He was still teaching drawing to the Gurney family, and was also a drawing teacher at Miss Heazel's Seminary in Tolls' Court, Briggs Lane, situated between Gentleman's Walk and Rampant Horse Street. By 1813 he was also the drawing master at the grammar school, and had little time to spend on his own painting.

In 1816 there was a huge row between Crome and his best friend, Ladbrooke. Their differences were over the Norwich Society. There was usually some money left over after the exhibitions, and it had been the custom to use the proceeds for a Society supper either once a fortnight or once a month. Bob Ladbrooke felt that the money should be spent on the purchase of casts, so the members of the Society could study them, and to make the Society more of a school. Crome preferred the suppers – and carried the vote. So Ladbrooke set up the 'Norfolk and Norwich Society of Artists' and exhibited on Theatre Street next to the Shakespeare Tavern (formerly on the site of the Forum). But the rival venture failed, and three years later Bob's school gave up exhibiting and its members (though not Bob himself) drifted back to the Norwich Society.

As well as painting, Crome worked as a picture restorer. He was paid £40, plus seven guineas in expenses, to restore and repair civic portraits in St Andrew's Hall, and cleaned them again in 1820 for a fee of twelve guineas. He also loved collecting pictures –

possibly under the influence of his patron Harvey – and was in debt to the Gurneys for more than £220 in 1812. He held a three-day sale in Yarmouth to clear the debt, and by 1815 he had more than £800 in his bank account.

On 14 April 1821, Crome was preparing a large canvas for a sketch of Wroxham Regatta. He came down with a fever and Fred Crome wrote to Dawson Turner on 21 April: 'My father's disorder has so much gained ground that there is not the least hope of him . . . he is seldom easy unless I am by his side.' At the same time, John Berney Crome wrote to Bob Ladbrooke and told him that Crome was dying. His erstwhile friend came to see him and, according to Henry Ladbrooke, Crome 'was quite sensible and expressed his great delight to see him. I need not say that they heartily exchanged forgiveness'.

Legend has it that just before Crome died, he put his hand out of bed and made movements as if he were painting: 'There, there. There's a touch, that will do, now another – that's it.' He then lost consciousness, and five minutes before the end, he said, 'Oh Hobbema! My dear Hobbema, how I have loved you.'

He died aged only 53 and was buried in St George's church in Colegate. His will was proved in November 1821 and he left the lease of the house to Phoebe, plus her choice of its contents. His sons were left £100 each at the age of 21, and his daughters £200, though if they married earlier than 21 without their mother's consent, they would have to wait until their twenty-first birthday before they could inherit the money. John Berney Crome and Frederick Crome were allowed to choose two pictures each. The remainder of his estate was to be sold and then held in trust with Phoebe receiving the income; at her death this would be divided between the children equally.

The sale of his collection ran to 750 lots; books, pictures, portfolios and crockery. The proceeds were nearly £740 plus another £260 from fees and the sales of pictures outstanding at his death. Less than fifty years later, his pictures were fetching more than £1,000 at auction.

As for his family, John Berney Crome became insolvent and had to sell the contents of the house; Emily taught drawing and painted flowers; William painted but lived in poverty in London; Joseph (born 1810) held 'a public appointment' and was said to be 'a good copyist'; and Michael, the baby of the family, became a dancing master but died penniless in London. Although the Cromes died out, Old Crome's legacy lives on in his paintings; these are moody moonlight scenes which capture the beauty of our city.

3

THE MOST FAMOUS PUFFER IN BRITAIN

Stephen John Fry is a man of many parts; actor, comic, writer, librettist, narrator, broadcaster, columnist and director. Though he is also a man of extremes. How else could a boy whose IQ score at the age of 12 indicated he was 'approaching genius' (he also won his school's Senior Greek Prize at the same age) go on to fail his A levels and spend three months in prison for petty theft? And how could a boy able to read at 3, and write at 4, never learn his times table? Fry is hard to pigeonhole. He flies his own biplane, he's six feet four and a half inches tall, collects teddy bears (and is regarded as 'Britain's favourite teddy bear') – and claims the record for using the F-word the most times on one live television broadcast. Oh, and his London house has two trees growing through the middle of it!

Although he wasn't born in Norwich – he was born on 24 August 1957 in Hampstead, middle child of the physicist and inventor Alan Fry and his wife Marianne – Fry grew up in Norfolk and remembers seeing *The Great Race* at the Gaumont in Norwich on his eighth birthday. His education in a Norwich college led to his award of a scholarship to Cambridge University, and nowadays he divides his time between West Hampstead and a country house in Norfolk where he writes.

Fry is also a regular supporter of Norwich City Football Club. And he puts his money where his mouth is; in 2002 he bought shares in City following the collapse of ITV Digital, saying, 'After the court judgement on ITV Digital it's a wonderful opportunity to be able to support a club that you love, by buying shares at whatever level.'

Fry began his education at Chesham Prep School in Buckinghamshire, where something happened that gave him his distinctive appearance: he tripped over in the playground and broke his nose. After his sister Joanna was born in 1965, the Frys moved to Norfolk. Fry then attended primary school in Cawston for a year. In his autobiography, *Moab Is My Washpot*, Fry dates his first lie for the sake of it to this school. It happened when he couldn't face taking the results of a spelling test to the head and told the teacher he'd left it on the head's desk, but told the head that he'd lost the sheet. He'd actually screwed it up and put it in a friend's wellie.

When he was 7 years old, Fry was sent to Stouts Hill School in Stroud, 200 miles away. Though he didn't have an easy time of it; an asthma attack when climbing the school's lime trees landed him in bed for two days, and he later broke his arm while seesawing with a friend. He also had a habit of speaking too quickly so that no one could understand him, though the school solved the problem by finding him an elocution teacher.

What they couldn't solve was his petty theft. Fry stole money from friends in the school changing-rooms. He also had a predilection for stealing sweets and, on one occasion, he even filched confiscated sweets from the headmaster's study. The head later found an unstamped parcel that Fry inadvertently left on the post tray, and told him off for it, although he never discovered the theft of the sweets. He called the boy into his office and said Fry would go far, as he had 'colossal nerve'!

From Stroud, Fry went to Uppingham School in Rutland, where he discovered comedy; his early influences were Wodehouse, Vivian Stanshall and Conan Doyle. Again he proved his precocity. He was expected to take his O levels at the age of 14, his A levels at 16 and go to university at 17. But he was sent down from school when he was caught stealing money from his house matron's handbag. His parents took him to a psychiatrist in London, who diagnosed him as having 'developmental delay': he was clever, but emotionally immature. Fry spent time at home, where his father taught him maths. He then took his O levels and got an unclassified in physics, mainly because he drew pictures and wrote smart comments in answer to the questions!

Fry chose to do English, French and Ancient History for A level;

but he was finally expelled from Uppingham in November 1972. He had permission to go to London with his friend Jo Woods, to attend a Sherlock Holmes Society meeting and stay in London for three days. Instead, Fry and Woods went to the cinema, and stayed in London for four days. After the difficulties he'd already had at school, Uppingham had had enough, and what they saw as a show of defiance was the last straw. They threw him out.

From Uppingham, Fry went to the Paston School in North Walsham in 1973. The school insisted that he should retake his O levels in 1974, then 'think about' A levels. Considering how bright Fry was, this was an insult. No wonder he hated it there and played truant for the next term and a half, smoking and playing pinball in the local cafés. The school promptly told him to leave. From there, Fry went to King's Lynn as a weekly boarder at the Norfolk College of Art and Technology. Again, his teachers weren't perceptive; the principal said that, with Fry's record of expulsion and truancy, there was no point in him trying for Oxbridge.

Aged 17 and increasingly miserable, he tried to kill himself. He took a cocktail of asthma medicine and aspirin; but his brother Roger heard him being sick and he was rushed to the Norfolk and Norwich hospital. He survived the attempt but was still unmotivated at college; he didn't even bother turning up to some of his A level papers.

And he didn't stay to find out the results. He ran away from home and went back to Chesham, to stay with family friends Amanda and Victoria Brooke. At this point, he stole their father's Diner's Club card and went on a spending spree. He started off in London, staying at the Imperial Hotel and spending his days in the American Bar at the Ritz. Then he went to the Cotswolds and stole an Access card, headed to Reading and got extremely drunk on his eighteenth birthday. His parents were frantic and asked the police to list him as a missing person. And still he didn't contact home, a pattern of behaviour that would be repeated years later. He went from Reading to Swindon, where he shopped with the stolen credit card and bought some shoes, then stole a cheap watch.

When he got back to the hotel, the police were waiting for him.

They told him that signing a false name was forgery; he could go down for five years. The magistrates remanded him to a prison for young offenders in Pucklechurch. Two weeks later, at the preliminary hearing, he pleaded guilty in court to one theft, and to three counts of 'by deception dishonestly obtaining pecuniary advantage'. Perhaps to punish himself, he refused bail and spent another seven weeks in Pucklechurch until his trial, when he was sentenced to two years probation.

This was when Fry turned his life around. As soon as he left Pucklechurch, he enrolled at City College in Norwich to undertake a one-year course of A levels in English, French and History of Art. The head of arts' admissions reviewed Fry's application and told him that he was too late, because the English and History of Art classes were full. The reason, of course, that Fry wasn't able to enrol earlier was because he was in court. He explained this, and said that he wanted to do those A levels and S levels so he could apply to Cambridge to read English. Fry also offered to pay one of the college staff to invigilate while he took the Cambridge entrance exam. He followed it up with the confident prediction that if he could do the courses he wanted, he would get a place to read English at Queens' College, Cambridge. The college authorities relented. Fry got his A and S levels, as predicted, then sat the Cambridge entrance exam in November, when he was the only one in the room apart from the invigilator! And then he got a telegram saying he'd won a scholarship to Queens' College.

After teaching at prep school for a year, Fry went up to Cambridge in 1979. While he was there, he became a member of the Cherubs drinking club and developed a taste for fine wines. When he could afford it, he bought extremely expensive vintages; on one occasion, after university, he shared an £860 bottle of 1955 Petrus with Julian Barnes. As well as joining the Cherubs, Fry joined Footlights, where he met Hugh Laurie. Fry appeared in more than thirty plays while he was at Cambridge, and wrote his first play (*Latin! or Tobacco and Boys*) in 1980, which won a Fringe First at the Edinburgh Festival in the same year.

Fry told his parents he was gay, then graduated with an upper second in English in 1981. The same year, he started writing with Hugh Laurie, including work on Footlights revues. The partnership has lasted spectacularly as they have also worked together on acclaimed television series such as *Jeeves and Wooster*, *A Bit of Fry and Laurie* and *Blackadder*.

In 1984, Fry rewrote *Me and My Girl*. The original stage musical was written by Douglas Furber, Arthur Rose and Noel Gay for the popular 1930's variety star, Lupino Lane. It opened in London in 1937, and ran for two years and almost 1,700 performances before the theatres were closed due to the outbreak of war. It was the first musical ever televised (in May 1939) and was filmed as *Lambeth Walk*; and then it fell into obscurity. Noel Gay's son, Richard Armitage, spent years searching for the original score and script. He asked Fry to rewrite and update it. Fry did so, and the musical opened in Leicester's Haymarket Theatre in December 1984. Fry hoped that it might run for six months and cover its costs, but what happened then must have been beyond his wildest dreams. The musical broke box office records, transferred to London's Adelphi Theatre and ran for 8 years (3,303 performances). It hit Broadway in 1986 and ran there for three and a half years (1,420 performances). The script earned Fry a nomination for a Tony award in 1987 and made him a millionaire before he was 30.

Fry's television work, radio voice-overs and acting career took off. He starred in three series of *Jeeves and Wooster* and also as Melchett in the *Blackadder* series, to critical acclaim. He also received accolades from the academic world; in 1995 he became rector of Dundee University and was also given an honorary doctorate by them. Life was sweet.

And then the tide turned. In 1995, Fry got mediocre reviews for his role in Simon Gray's stage play *Cell Mates*. He considered suicide and actually trailed a hosepipe from the exhaust of his car through the window, but then couldn't bring himself to turn on the ignition. Instead, without telling anyone where he was going – exactly as he'd done as a 17-year-old – he ran away. He took a ferry to Zeebrugge and made his way to Germany. Then he disappeared again and was finally spotted in Bruges. Finally, he sent a fax to his agent, saying, 'I'm a silly old fool and I don't deserve this attention.'

His father picked him up, and Fry went into a mental hospital for a while, followed by a spell in America. Then in 1996, life started looking up again. Fry met Daniel Cohen, twelve years his junior, after sixteen years of celibacy and promptly fell in love.

In 1997, the University of East Anglia awarded him an honorary Doctorate of Letters – at the same time as Salman Rushdie – and in 1997 he made his debut on the big screen, playing the title role in *Wilde*. It won him the 1998 Seattle International Film Festival Golden Space Needle Award for Best Actor. The same film also netted him nominations for the 1999 Golden Globe for Best Performance by an Actor in a Motion Picture, and the 1999 Golden Satellite Award for the Best Actor in a Motion Picture (Drama). His film career has gone from strength to strength, and has included roles in projects as diverse as *Thunderpants* and *Gosford Park*, which won him a Screen Actors' Guild Award for Outstanding Performance by the Cast of a Theatrical Motion Picture in 2002.

His writing career has also flourished. His first novel, *The Liar*, appeared in 1991 and held the number-one spot on the best-seller lists for months. He followed that in 1992 with *Paperweight*, a collection of essays and other writings. His second novel, *The Hippopotamus*, was published in 1994, followed by *Making History* in 1996 and *The Stars' Tennis Balls* in 2001. All received critical acclaim, as did his autobiography, *Moab Is My Washpot*. He also published a diary, *Rescuing the Spectacled Bear*, about his visit to Peru to track Paddington Bear's roots and to rescue a Spectacled Bear, one of the world's most-endangered species.

At the time of writing in early 2003, Fry is working on his debut as a director for a Film Four production – *Bright Young Things*, based on Evelyn Waugh's *Vile Bodies*. Though he wouldn't be Stephen Fry without a hint of naughtiness. He was caught speeding in November 2001 and ended up with six points on his licence; late in 2002 he was caught speeding on the A11 at ninety-nine miles per hour on his way to the radio show *Sorry I Haven't a Clue*, for which he was late. He ended up with five points and a £300 fine, so he wasn't quite banned from driving, and was thus able to watch Norwich City play over Christmas.

In 2003 Fry became the thirty-ninth person to receive the Pipe Smoker of the Year award from the Pipe Smokers' Council. Though Fry didn't start by smoking tobacco; when he was 14, he borrowed his father's pipe and started smoking tea, because he'd heard that 'it gave you a buzz'. Fry was delighted with the award, saying, 'I am the most famous puffer in Britain – and you can take the "er" off that.'

Perhaps Fry's own words are best to sum him up. 'It is quite difficult to feel that I am placed somewhere between Alan Bennett and the Queen Mother, a sort of public kitten.'

4

DELIA

Although Delia Smith wasn't born in Norwich – she was born in Woking on 18 June 1941 – her support for and directorship of Norwich City Football Club has made her very much associated with the city. And the *Sunday Times* list of the most powerful people in 1999 placed her second in East Anglia.

In Delia, we have someone whose first name is a included in a dictionary definition. She gained an entry in *Collins Dictionary* in 2001 with a 'Delia dish' ('from a recipe or in the style of cooking of British cookery writer Delia Smith') and the 'Delia effect' (when there's a rush for an ingredient or piece of equipment she's recommended, such as cranberries and omelette pans), as well as 'Delia power' and 'doing a Delia'. Hardly surprising from someone who has sold more than fifteen million books and made an estimated £24 million from cookery.

Born into an era of rationing, Delia refers to memories of home-made cakes, biscuits and preserves when her mother and grandmother spent a day a week baking. She lived next door to her grandparents, Marshall and Ellen Smith; Ellen was a good cook and Delia's mother Etty loved cooking too, and her Welsh grandfather William Pugh used to take her mushrooming.

In 1946 she went to Upland Infant School in Bexleyheath, and was teased for being snobby as she spoke well and was smartly dressed. She was good at religious education but other than that wasn't academic; she failed her eleven plus and went to Bexleyheath School. Everyone expected her to do what everyone else did: get a job in a shop, marry a local boy and settle in Bexleyheath. However, her parents split up when she was 14 and this perhaps influenced her to move away and do something different. She left school in 1957 without qualifications and decided to work in London, though not in cooking. Her first job was in a travel agency answering the phone and then, in 1960, she left home and found work as a junior stylist in a London salon.

In 1962 she discovered what she really wanted to do, when she went out with friends for a meal at The Singing Chef in Connaught Street, in the West End. She tried chef Leo Evans's signature dish, omelette soufflé flambé, and loved it so much that she told him she wanted to learn how to make it. Evans gave her a job as washer-up with the promise of promotion to kitchen assistant. She also did some waitressing and within a couple of weeks was promoted to kitchen assistant. She took a notebook into work and made notes about everything Evans did, and one of the first dishes she learned was roast duck with sour cherry sauce. Leo Evans taught her to be methodical, to take things step by step and explained everything with specific instructions – something which has become the hallmark of a Delia recipe today.

Around that time, Delia also started working as a stylist in a photographic studio and as a make-up artist for television commercials. When someone dropped a pie they were about to film she told everyone not to worry, because she could make another, and she did. The story spread and questions started to be asked about whether she would be able to present a television programme, though nothing came of it.

She then had a stint working for Madame Maurer's restaurant in London to gain more experience, and followed that up by working as a live-in cook for professor Simon Yudkin, his wife Cicely and their son John in Harley Street. She overheard lots of conversations about how bad English food was, compared with French, but she also learnt that English food in the eighteenth century was the best in the world. It fired her imagination and she bought a ticket for the reading room of the British Museum and researched the history of English cooking. She tried out some old recipes with great success and started thinking about food writing as a career. She could see a gap in the market between the dull 'budget' recipes published in magazines and the expensive, sophisticated recipes. She was determined to write a book, but had no experience in publishing and no idea how to take the project forward.

The break came in 1969, when she met Deborah Owen, who was just starting out as a literary agent. Delia helped her to cook dishes for her new husband, Dr David Owen, who would later become Foreign Secretary and then leader of the Social Democratic Party. Deborah Owen in turn heard of an opening at the *Daily Mirror*, which was about to launch a new magazine, and recommended Delia. Delia couldn't type or spell, and her first effort was terrible, but the editor, Mike Molloy, gave her a chance and told her to try again. Her first piece included recipes for kipper pâté, beef in beer and cheesecake, and it was a success.

Mike Molloy was also instrumental in another part of Delia's life; he introduced her to his deputy, Michael Wynn Jones. Delia had already had her heart broken in the mid-sixties, when the Catholic missionary she fell in love with, Louis Alexander, went away to study philosophy in the Netherlands and decided to become a priest. She and Michael were complete opposites: he'd been to public school and read Greats at Oxford; she'd left a secondary modern without qualifications; he was agnostic whereas she was a devout Catholic; and Delia herself is on record as saying that Michael is very laid back and thoughtful whereas she wants everything now. But they fell in love. He took her home to meet his parents, and also introduced her to something else that would become a very important part of her life – Norwich City Football Club.

They moved in together at Primrose Hill. Then in 1971 they were made redundant and bought a cottage in Combs, near Stowmarket. They married in September, and Delia's career really took off. She started working for the *Evening Standard* and wrote her first book, *How to Cheat at Cooking*.

Then she had a stroke of luck when she was recommended for a job in television. Paul Fox approved her proposal in his last half-hour as controller of BBC One, before leaving for Yorkshire

Television. The first series of *Family Fare* was aired in September 1973; the first programme was shot without editing or breaks, in a studio with no cooking or washing up facilities! Although Delia was very nervous, and suffered from eczema and hives because of the stress, it worked. Her next book, in 1973, was *Recipes from Country Inns and Restaurants*; Delia said simply that her 'ideas are for the ordinary housewife who likes cooking'.

Following her success on *Family Fare*, Delia was asked to do the cookery slot on the BBC regional programme, *Look East*. She did weekly five-minute slots starting in 1975, which were filmed in Norwich and piped straight to Birmingham. There was no editing facility, so it was like doing a live performance.

But then came the backlash. In 1976, Aubrey Singer, the new controller at the BBC, decided that Delia was 'not sexy enough' and moved her programme to the late-night BBC Two education slot. Delia still had her *Look East* slots but it wasn't quite the same. Personal sadness followed when she and Michael found they were unable to have children. And some critics argued that she was extravagant; her response was to write *Delia Smith's Frugal Food*. As if that wasn't enough to silence them, she also donated all the royalties from the book to Christian Aid and the Catholic Fund for Overseas Development.

The late-night education slot had made Delia think carefully about what she was doing, so when she started writing her *Cookery Course*, she decided to go back to basics. She wanted to tell people why as well as how; for example, why choux pastry puffs up (it's all to do with the water in the pastry turning to steam and pushing the pastry up) and what actually happens to the mixture when you bake a cake.

1981 saw another new direction when Delia did an interview with Sue McGregor on *Home on Sunday* about her faith. She then wrote three books on religious themes: *A Feast for Lent* (the royalties from which she donated to Great Ormond Street Hospital), followed by *A Feast for Advent* and *A Journey into God*.

Through the 1980s (and the advent of nouvelle cuisine), Delia didn't do much writing on cookery, but then in 1990 she brought out *Delia Smith's Christmas*. It broke sales records, and the whole of Europe sold out of liquid glucose because of her recipe for chocolate truffle torte! The *Summer Collection* followed in 1993, and she was awarded an OBE in 1994. The *Summer Collection* had done well, selling a million copies by 1995, but the *Winter Collection*, published in 1995, completely eclipsed it, selling half a million copies in only a week. The book also led to the great cranberry shortage; there was a bad harvest that year anyway, but there were seven recipes in the collection which used cranberries. Given the book's huge sales, it was obvious there would be a run on cranberries, and there simply weren't enough berries to go round. In 1997, the University of East Anglia awarded her an honorary degree of Doctor of Letters, but she turned down the offer of a peerage in the same year from Tony Blair.

She became a director of Norwich City Football Club in November 1996; at the time, Delia said their catering was the worst in Britain and one of the first things she did was to change the caterers. She took the operation in-house in 1999 and opened Delia's City Brasserie in 2000, with all profits going to the club. By the end of 1997, she and her husband owned the majority of shares in the club.

Delia changed the players' kit in 1998 and commissioned Bruce Oldfield to design it. But it was all yellow (some people even dubbed it 'mustard' yellow, particularly as City were sponsored by Colman's at the time) and it was very unpopular with the fans, who wanted the Canaries' traditional green shorts back. In the end it went to a vote and fans had a chance to hold up a card to show whether they wanted green shorts or yellow. Delia held out for yellow, but the sea of green swamped her. She managed to keep Oldfield's designs for the staff in the Brasserie, though!

And then there was another Delia backlash. Delia had annoyed the cookery establishment, which snubbed her for an award and put the *River Café Cookbook* ahead of her *Winter Collection* (despite the fact that the *River Café Cookbook* had comparatively low sales of 50,000). And when she launched *How to Cook* in October 1998, it sparked a row with Gary Rhodes, who said it was 'insulting and offensive'.

The public didn't care; the book sold like hot cakes and Delia followed it up with a second series. But then she decided to take a break: thirty years of books and television had left her feeling 'like a machine' and she wanted to concentrate on football for a while. This included paying for new kitchens at Carrow Road out of her own pocket and helping to bail out the club when, for one month, it couldn't meet the players' wages. Though things became turbulent at Carrow Road, with the club doing very badly in the 2000/01 season and manager Bryan Hamilton walking out.

Another row started when Delia turned 60, and confessed that she was sick of the St Delia image. 'I'm not prim, I am a bit of a bitch,' she told an interviewer, adding that she sings rude songs about the opposition at Carrow Road (though she doesn't join in the ones that include swearing). And finally she told us what she thought of the other television foodies: 'Actually, I hate Gary Rhodes' programmes and I think that Anthony Worrall Thompson is worse; he is dreadful, just repulsive . . . the show that he is on is the most disgusting programme on television.' She added that Jilly Goolden was 'awful' and Michael Barry was 'all sweaty palms'. Worrall Thompson wasn't bothered; he replied that her comments were probably because Norwich were doing so badly, and added that she had every right to have a go at those who'd had a go at her, which included him and Gary Rhodes. And on the repulsiveness issue? 'I find her quite attractive actually and she gets more beautiful as she gets older.'

How to Cook Book 3 followed in 2001, and *Delia's Vegetarian Collection* in October 2002. Although she believes in meat and enjoys eating it, she wanted to bring together a collection of the vegetarian recipes she really rates. She has her finger firmly on the pulse of what the public wants, and has even rewritten her original *Cookery Course* to reduce the levels of fat and sugar, reflecting the demand for healthy eating. Though she isn't totally convinced about organic food, and has pointed out in interviews that she always picks the freshest food (which is often the non-organic variety).

As for the future, Delia has said in recent interviews that she would quite like to do a menu book. Now she's over 60, what about retirement? Delia is on record as saying that she'll slow down, 'just pick and choose' and 'start at ten and finish at four.' But the real blow for foodies came in January 2003, when she declared that she was 'reciped out'. She said, 'There will be no more television or books. This football club and these people are my life and I'm having fun and now I'm devoting myself to Norwich City.' Anthony Worrall Thompson called her 'the Volvo of cooking – safe, reliable but dull'. That reliability is precisely what her fans will miss, but Delia's reputation is set to grow in a different area. According to surveys in France, young French women regard cooking as tedious and don't even know where to start. So Delia may well have as big an impact across the Channel with her *La Cuisine Facile d'Aujourd'hui (Simple Cooking for Today)* as she's had here in Britain.

5

MISCARRIAGE OF JUSTICE?

The summer of 1999 saw a trial in Norwich which sparked a nationwide debate about the rights of householders to defend their own property: the case of Tony Martin.

Was he a maniac who used an illegal weapon against three burglars who didn't deserve the violent reception they got at his farmhouse? Tony Joynes, the uncle of burglar Fred Barras, said, 'He didn't deserve to die at 16 . . . If he'd been given a good hiding that would have been understandable. I don't agree with him breaking the law but he shouldn't have been shot.' Or was Martin simply defending himself after police failed time and time again to protect him against crime? The three burglars, after all, had more than a hundred convictions between them, and many believed they got exactly what they deserved. Joseph Fearon, the father of one of the burglars – Brendan Fearon – could see the other side of the story. He said that Martin 'was protecting his own property. It was his house, his home and they should never have been there. People have to be able to protect their own homes from burglary. People work hard for what they have got and it must be soul-destroying to have it snatched away.'

The question that was asked up and down the country was, 'What would you have done in Tony Martin's shoes?' Alone in an empty farmhouse after a spate of thefts and vandalism in the area, hearing a noise beneath you that meant you'd been targeted by thieves: would you have hit back?

Tony Martin owned an isolated farm – appropriately called 'Bleak House' – in the village of Emneth Hungate, near Wisbech. He lived in conditions approaching squalor, with his three Rottweiler dogs (Otto, Daniel and Bruno) and a huge collection of teddy bears.

He'd suffered from depression throughout his life, including the months prior to the night in question, and he slept fully clothed on top of his bed because he'd been burgled so many times. Martin had been abused as a child and feared being attacked, so he turned his home into a fortress. So when thieves targeted his farm, it made him feel more vulnerable and paranoid than the average person, though this evidence wasn't brought out at the original trial.

Martin had already been burgled in May 1999. And on 19 August 1999, three burglars came from Newark into Norfolk. Brendan Fearon was 32 years old and a father of three. He'd already accumulated four prison sentences and thirty-five court appearances for burglary, drug offences and offences against the person, the first being when he was only 14. Apparently he acted as a kind of uncle to 16-year-old Fred Barras and – although it's very hard to see the logic in this – only took him along to the burglary to 'keep him out of trouble'.

Fred Barras had been in trouble at the age of 12 for shoplifting, and was just 13 when he first appeared in court, to be convicted of two assaults, obtaining property by deception and forgery. At the time of the burglary, he already had twenty-eight convictions, including two for offences against the person, six for fraud and seven for theft, with two spells in young offenders' institutions. Indeed, he had a bail sheet in his pocket when his body was found; he'd been arrested on suspicion of theft just days before the raid on Bleak House.

Nor was Darren Bark, the getaway driver, an angel. He'd been released from prison only weeks earlier when his four-year sentence for antique theft had been halved; that was his second sentence for burglary, and he'd also appeared in court on fifty-two occasions on theft and assault charges.

Three burglars, all convicted of theft and assault, versus an old man who was mentally ill.

So what actually happened? Bark, the getaway driver, didn't actually go to the farm. Fearon and Barras approached the farm buildings, retreated from one of Martin's dogs along a path and forced their way into the house through a window. Fearon heard a noise and shone his torch towards the stairs. He saw Martin, who fired his Winchester pump-action shotgun down into the darkness, hitting Barras in the back and Fearon in the legs (Fearon later had nearly two hundred pieces of shot dug out of his legs). Fearon dragged himself out through the window again, then crawled to a nearby house. Barras crawled through the window and died in the nearby undergrowth.

At the trial, the prosecution claimed that Martin was waiting for the burglars in the dark on the ground floor of his home and had effectively 'executed' Barras. The first shot was actually fired from the stairs, but the defence wasn't sure about how to explain why a frightened man had come all the way downstairs to fire two more shots, so they let the point pass.

The prosecution also argued that Martin was an angry man, who had violent views about burglars and especially about travellers – Barras was from a travellers' community – and claimed that Martin had once talked of 'putting gypsies in one of his fields surrounded by barbed wire and machine gunning them'. This ignores the fact that Martin himself had been a traveller at one point; when his imagination was fired by his uncle's stories of travelling the world, Martin went to Liverpool, got on a boat and went to Australia, Singapore and New Zealand. He said of his trip later: 'I lived in a car, sleeping rough and just kept on the move. I was never fussy about jobs, got one purely so I could eat. Often I worked on farms, including a stint as a sheep shearer, and it fired an early enthusiasm for farming.'

Martin's account of what happened that night was that while he was asleep he was woken by sounds from downstairs. Realising that someone was in the house he grabbed his gun. He gave a vivid and moving account of what happened next in an interview with David Winnings of the *Eastern Daily Press*,

> Look, I don't agree with shooting people. It's not something I take lightly. On the night of the burglary I was a terrified man alone in the house . . . I was disturbed by noises outside and didn't know how many people were out there . . . I knew somebody was down there now because there were lights. I walked out of the bedroom on to the landing and went down the stairs . . . this light shone in

my eyes . . . I couldn't stand it any longer and then I just let the gun off . . . then ran upstairs. The police say I shouldn't have had a gun because my gun licence had been revoked . . . But is it right that you should live in your own house in fear? I didn't know a boy had died and that I had taken a life until the police informed me on Saturday.

Two days after the shooting, Martin was arrested at a hotel in Wisbech. Detectives then searched the farm and found the body of Fred Barras in the undergrowth. Two days later, Martin was charged with murder, wounding with intent and possessing an illegally-held pump-action shotgun. He appeared before magistrates the following day at King's Lynn, and was given bail on 7 September, on condition he stayed at a safe house outside Norfolk. The following day saw a packed public meeting in Emneth village hall. The villagers, angered by the rising crime wave and the apparent impotence and indifference of the authorities, shouted down both police and politicians.

On the side of the burglars, hundreds attended the funeral of Fred Barras on 9 September at Newark, where the vicar said there should be no thoughts of revenge and appealed for calm. But travellers had put a £50,000 bounty on Tony Martin's head, so he was sent to Norwich prison for his own safety, then bailed on 17 September to a secret address. Three days later the getaway driver, Darren Bark, jumped bail, afraid that the travellers in Newark would blame him for Barras's death. He was rearrested in Torquay.

On 8 November 1999, Brendan Fearon appeared before King's Lynn magistrates, charged with conspiring to burgle Tony Martin's home. Meanwhile, police were spending £20,000 a month to protect Bleak House, which was to be used as an exhibit at the trial.

In April 2000, Martin stood trial at Norwich Crown Court. The prosecution stated that the three key areas in the case were the distance between the parties when the gun was fired, the number of shots and whether or not anything was said or done by either party. In other words, where was Martin, what was he doing, and what was he aware of at the time?

At the end of the eight-day trial on 19 April 2000, the jury took nine hours and thirty-six minutes to decide that Martin hadn't shot Barras in self-defence. The 10–2 majority verdict was that he was guilty of murdering Fred Barras, though he was cleared of attempting to murder Fearon and possessing a shotgun with intent to danger life. The judge gave him a life sentence, plus ten years for wounding Fearon. Nicholas Crampton, one of the Norwich-based solicitors for the Crown Prosecution Service, said later that if Martin had fired fewer shots, the charge would probably have been reduced.

The jury clearly believed he fired in anger, and so brought in a guilty verdict. Though in one television poll soon after the verdict, 85 per cent of those who voted said they believed the jury had got it wrong. And in a leaked memo from Downing Street, shortly after the poll, Tony Blair admitted he wondered if he'd lost touch with the feelings of the people of Britain, and he clearly had no idea how strongly people felt about the Martin case. Lord Woolf, the Lord Chief Justice, claimed judges were being forced to pass inappropriate sentences because Parliament had taken away their discretion in some cases by imposing mandatory sentences; whether you were a mercy killer or a serial killer, you'd receive the same sentence. Life.

Just over a week after the trial, a juror called a local radio station and claimed she'd been threatened. She said she'd dialled 999 during the trial as she thought she was being followed, and other people had also spoken to the judge in private because they felt intimidated. However, her claims weren't broadcast by the station, and the Lord Chancellor's department said it hadn't received any formal complaints from jurors.

Even so, Martin's lawyer Nick Makin lodged an appeal, arguing that witnesses and jurors had been intimidated, rendering the conviction unsafe. Meanwhile, feelings were running high in Norfolk. Rural communities said they felt threatened by crime and had lost confidence in the police to such an extent that they were prepared to take the law into their own hands. In response, Norfolk's Chief Constable Ken Williams warned people not to go down the road of American-style gun-law culture.

In August 2000, Martin sacked his legal team and appointed a new solicitor, James Saunders, on the grounds that his original solicitor was a civil lawyer who specialised in commercial, rather than criminal, law. On 1 November 2000, Fearon and Bark were jailed for their part in the robbery. Fearon was given three years and Bark forty-two months. In February 2001, Martin's new solicitor stated that he wanted the murder conviction reduced to manslaughter, on the grounds that Martin had a history of health problems. Then, in April 2001, probation officers advised Fearon that he was a victim of crime and therefore entitled to be consulted about the terms of Martin's parole. Again, people across the country scratched their heads. If someone burgles you, even if you take a stand against the burglar, how can the burglar be a victim?

In June 2001, Fred Barras's father – who had an awful lot to say about how wrong it was to shoot people – was jailed for fourteen years after taking part in an armed robbery. An armed robbery in which a female security guard was tied up.

In July 2001, Martin's appeal was put back to give the prosecution more time. In August, Fearon was released after serving just half his sentence, claiming that he was going straight from then on and still had nightmares about that night in Emneth. Bark was released in September 2001, after serving even less of his sentence. Within weeks he was in Sheffield Crown Court, where he admitted burglary, causing actual bodily harm and making threats to kill.

In October 2001, Martin's appeal was heard, with new evidence about his mental health. The appeal court was informed that Martin had a paranoid personality disorder and his mental responsibility was therefore 'substantially diminished' when he pulled the trigger. Ballistics expert Dr Graham Renshaw also took the stand and gave evidence that Martin was coming down the stairs when he shot the burglars – he wasn't lying in wait in a booby-trapped farm. But Lord Woolf rejected claims that Martin had acted in self-defence and used no more force than was reasonable to protect himself and his property. He said, 'Martin used a firearm which he knew he was not entitled to have in a manner which was wholly unjustified.'

So was he not entitled to protect himself? Woolf again: 'Mr Martin was entitled to use reasonable force to protect himself and his home, but the jury were surely correct in coming to their judgment that he wasn't acting reasonably in shooting one of the intruders, who happened to be 16, dead and seriously injuring the other.'

At the end of October, Martin's murder conviction was reduced to manslaughter and his sentence was cut to five years. The wounding charges were reduced to three years, the sentences to be served concurrently. He wasn't given leave to appeal to the House of Lords against his conviction. He was eligible for parole in October 2002, but at the time of writing (in early 2003) he is still in prison. It was thought that he would be released in January 2003 but he continues to serve his time at Highpoint, a low-security prison in Suffolk.

The parole board that considered his case reported that Martin gets on well with staff and other prisoners, but added that his views about protecting his property were entrenched. In consequence, it believes there is a strong likelihood he would do exactly the same thing again and, for that reason, didn't recommend parole.

Martin – known as prisoner BH9000 – has already been in five different jails: Norwich, Bullingdon in Oxfordshire (where another prisoner tried to set fire to him), Gartree near Leicester, Pentonville and now Highpoint. He has said that he wants to return to Bleak House, 'depending on the season' and 'when the mood is right'. His dogs are currently being looked after by friends and he clearly misses them. He says he will not buy another gun and would not take the law into his own hands again if faced with burglars. But there's still a £50,000 bounty on his head and the police believe they cannot guarantee his safety if he returns home. In fact, he may need to be moved abroad with a new identity for his own protection.

Martin might not have had a home anyway, because he might have had to sell his house to pay Fearon. Quite incredibly, in December 2002, Fearon sued Martin for up to £50,000 compensation for loss of earnings. He claimed he could not find work (this from a professional burglar), enjoy sex, or pursue his martial-arts hobbies of ju-jitsu and kickboxing. He admittted in the writ that he 'intended to burgle' Martin, even though he claimed originally that he only broke in to the farmhouse to evade Martin's dogs. Because of reading and writing difficulties, Fearon has 'only ever managed to find unskilled manual work' and is now 'at a disadvantage in the labour market' because of the injuries to his legs. He claimed that he became depressed and attempted suicide after the shooting, and now suffers post-traumatic stress syndrome. The incident has also instilled a fear of fireworks and watching shoot-outs on television, and he cries if someone dies in a film.

Incredibly, Fearon was awarded £5,000 by legal aid for his damages claim. He wasn't entitled to an award for criminal injuries, because he and Barras were carrying out a crime when Martin fired at them. But justice eventually prevailed: Fearon's case was thrown out by Nottingham Crown Court in April 2003, a result that may also dissuade Barras's family from bringing a civil case against Martin.

Martin wants to launch a counter-suit for the stress and fear inflicted by the burglar, but he will need £150,000 to cover the costs. In addition Makin, his original lawyer, blocked his legal aid, so that Martin is unable to pay his new lawyer. Makin is also suing Martin for alleged non-payment of fees.

After the appeal, Gillian Shephard, the Conservative MP for South-West Norfolk, said, 'I've never known a case that has aroused such national, indeed, international reaction. I cannot recall one that has produced a more unanimous feeling – Tony Martin should not have been convicted of murder.' She could have gone further and added: the law needs to be changed, so that burglars can't sue their own victims.

As for public opinion, perhaps the 7,500 Christmas cards Martin received in December 2002 speak for themselves.

6

WILL KEMP'S 'NINE DAIES MORRIS'

1599 saw Norwich at the centre of a drama between Shakespeare and his colleague, Will Kemp. Kemp, after a furious row, determined to prove that he and not Shakespeare was the public's favourite; he bet Shakespeare that he could dance from London to Norwich in nine days – and actually backed himself at odds of 3–1!

Accompanied by a Tom Slye (drummer and piper), William Bee (general servant) and George Spratt (a referee), Kemp danced his way to Norwich. The journey actually took a month because he had 'rest days', but the times that he danced were the only ones that were counted for the purpose of the bet.

According to Kemp's *Nine Daies Wonder*, on 'the first Monday in Lent, the close morning promising a clear day', 'Cavaliero Kemp' (as he termed himself) set off from the Lord Mayor's of London at just before seven in the morning. As he danced through the streets, people threw money at him and wished him well. He left Whitechapel and 'fair London' behind, then headed for Mile End, though he was followed by 'multitudes of Londoners' who either wanted to have a 'recreation at Stratford Bow with cream and cakes' or have a good laugh because they thought he would give up 'within a mile of Mile-End'. Kemp rested at Bow and just about resisted all the offers of a drink, then headed for Stratford Langton. The crowds there had prepared a bear-baiting for him, knowing that it was his favourite entertainment, but because of the crush he couldn't actually see the spectacle, only hear the roar of the bear and the snarling of the dogs. He continued to Ilford and rested there – again resisting a drink from a 'great spoon' which held 'above a quart' – before setting off from Ilford in moonlight and dancing to Romford.

A quarter of a mile outside Romford, he was too tired to go on and accepted the offer of a lift on a horse into town.

He rested at Romford for two days, where 'Londoners came hourly thither in great numbers to visit' him; and then on the Thursday morning returned to the place where he'd accepted the lift, then danced through to Brentwood, straining his hip on the way. At Brentwood, two cutpurses claimed that they were following Kemp because they'd laid wagers about his journey, but when the officers brought them to the inn where Kemp was staying, Kemp said he didn't know them but recognised one as a well-known London cutpurse. That evening, Kemp danced by moonlight to Ingatestone with about fifty followers.

On the Friday, Kemp danced to Chelmsford, 'not having past two hundred' people with him, 'being the least company that I had in the daytime between London and that place.' It took him an hour to work through the throng to his inn, where he rested, completely shattered. The next morning, he 'footed it three miles' towards Braintree but realised he needed to rest so returned to Chelmsford, again resisting temptation, 'for my only desire was to refrain [from] drink, and be temperate in my diet'. A 14-year-old girl asked him to dance the morris with her and their leaps and frolics lasted for an hour before Kemp needed a rest!

Monday of the second week saw the fourth day of Kemp's journey. It was a rough route, with thick woods on either side and a lane full of potholes where he found himself 'up to the waist' in mud and water half the time. Two of the people who'd followed him clearly annoyed him – 'one, a fine light fellow, would be still before me, the other ever at my heels' – and finally, when Kemp came to a huge puddle that couldn't be avoided, he leaped over it and landed up to his ankles at the far end, but one of his irritating followers got stuck in the middle and had to be helped out by his friend. The dousing was enough to make them swear they wouldn't dance with him 'for the next seven years'!

He reached Braintree at noon and stayed until Wednesday, dancing three miles on the Tuesday to ease his journey. On the

Wednesday, his fifth day of dancing, he danced to Sudbury, where a butcher offered to accompany him to Bury – but only made it halfway, saying he wouldn't go further for £100. Will's comment? 'Indeed my pace in dancing is not ordinary.' A woman in the audience with 'sides well larded, Every bone with fat flesh guarded' teased the exhausted butcher and said she would dance a mile with Kemp – so she tucked up her petticoat, the butcher 'garnished her thick short legs' with bells, and she danced to Melford with Kemp, who gave her a crown to buy a drink (as well as what he terms 'a skinful'!).

Kemp rested at Melford until the Saturday; on his sixth day of dancing, he danced to Clare, rested, then headed to Bury, taking a break at the Widow Everett's house. Again, he was received well by the town and was 'stayed seven times' before he could reach the inn where he was staying. But then there was a snowstorm, and he was forced to stay at Bury until the following Thursday.

On the Friday morning, his seventh day, he danced the ten miles to Thetford in three hours. He stayed there until the Monday morning, when Sir Edmund Rich gave him £5, and then danced to Rockland on the eighth day. The innkeeper there sounded quite a character – 'being armed at all points, from the cap to the codpiece, his black shoes shining, and made straight with copper buckles of the best, his garters in the fashion, and every garment fitting Corremsquandam (to use his own word)' – and stuttered at Will that he was 'very welcome . . . as welcome as the Queen's best greyhound'! From Rockland he danced to Hingham, where he stayed overnight.

The ninth day of dancing saw Kemp dancing from Hingham to Barford on the Wednesday morning, then from Barford to Norwich itself. But there were so many people at St Giles' Gate that he stopped and rode into the city, deciding to finish his dance at a 'better opportunity'. Roger Wiler, the Mayor, suggested that Kemp should finish his morris on the following Saturday. Kemp stayed with various aldermen and the Mayor, then on the Saturday finished his dance.

He returned out through St Giles' Gate to where he'd ridden

into the city, and came back in through St Stephen's Gate, where Thomas Gilbert welcomed him on behalf of Norwich with an acrostic rhyme:

With hart, and hand, among the rest,
Especially you welcome are:
Long looked for, as welcome guest,
Come now at last you be from farre.
Of most within the Citty sure,
Many good wishes you have had.
Each one did pray you might indure,
With courage good the match you made.
Intend they did with gladsome hearts,
Like your well willers, you to meete:
Know you also they'll doe their parts,
Eyther in field or house to greete
More you then any with you came,
Procur'd thereto with trump and fame.

The city Whifflers parted the crowds so Kemp could dance through to the market place, where the City Waits met him with music. They certainly impressed Kemp, who said of them: 'few cities in our realm have the like, none better . . . Besides their excellency in wind instruments, their rare cunning on the viol and violin, their voices be admirable.'

More and more people crowded round him at the market place, and then Kemp embarrassed one of the city maidens, whom he obviously thought a country wench 'but newly crept into the fashion of long-waisted petticoats tied with points'. She'd only tied the petticoat on with one point of lace in the front, so when Kemp landed with one foot on her skirts, the impact broke the lace and her petticoat fell off! 'Though her smock were coarse, it was cleanly' he noticed – and the poor girl had to recover her petticoat 'from unruly boys' and, 'looking before like one that had the green sickness, now had she her cheeks all coloured with scarlet.'

Kemp leaped over the churchyard wall at St John Maddermarket so that he could reach the mayor's house; but George Spratt, his overseer, had lost sight of him in the crowds and made him dance the last quarter of a mile again on the Tuesday.

The buskins Kemp wore and had danced in from London were nailed to the wall of the Guildhall and the mayor gave him 'five pounds in Elizabeth Angels' and forty shillings a year and also made him a freeman of the merchant venturers.

Kemp wrote his account of his journey in *Nine Daies Wonder*, and addressed a postscript to 'My notable Shakerags . . . I know you to be a sort of witless beetlehead, that can understand nothing but what is knocked into your scalps' and explained he knew who the author of scurrilous ballads had been, 'a penny poet whose first making was the miserable stolen story of Macdoel, or Macdobeth, or Macsomewhat: for I am sure a Mac it was, though I never had the maw to see it.'

His gravestone in Southwark mentions his feat – 'Welcome from Norwich, Kempe all joy to see, Thy safe return morriscoed lustily.'

Four hundred years later, in 2000 – due to a quirk in the calendar, it was 2000 rather than 1999 – the 127-mile route was danced as a morris relay by morris clubs in the eastern region, with each club completing a 'leg'. They started from London's Royal Exchange on 15 April and reached Norwich on the Saturday, knocking a day off Kemp's record and not stopping for rest days! Two musicians and six dancers did the whole route, including 20-year-old Bethan McLachlan from Norwich who played her recorder the whole way.

The dancers performed in Chapelfield gardens, then presented Lord Mayor Doug Underwood with a scroll before going to St John Maddermarket and leaping over the wall in true Kemp style, then joining a feast and a ceilidh in St Andrews' Hall.

7

DISASTER AT THORPE

The evening of 10 September 1874 saw one of the worst railway accidents of the century on the Great Eastern Railway Company's line between Norwich and Brundall. It was the first ever accident on that stretch of line during the twenty-six years it had been controlled by telegraph, despite it being extremely busy with passengers and goods traffic. According to the *Norfolk Chronicle and Norwich Gazette*, the safety record was so good (despite the trains always being late!) that the Great Eastern Railway was known as 'slow but sure'.

Nobody had any idea that 10 September was going to change that for good.

A new branch line was about to be completed to make the single-line rail into double track, but it was too late for the 9.10 express train from Norwich to Yarmouth, which had a head-on collision with the mail train from Yarmouth.

Usually, the 8.40 mail train from Yarmouth stopped at Brundall until the 9.10 express train from Norwich had arrived at the station, and then was sent on. But William Platford, the station master at Brundall, had received instructions saying that if the train was late at Thorpe (as it had frequently been in the last few months, it was twenty-three minutes late that night), he could send the Yarmouth train straight down.

That night, Brundall had a telegraph saying that he could send the Yarmouth train down. Platford sent a reply saying he would send the train to Norwich.

But minutes later, the staff at Thorpe station realised that the trains were going to meet each other head-on in the middle of the single line, and there was no way of stopping either train or getting a message to them. It was the first head-on rail crash in Norfolk for a quarter of a century; and if the accident had happened just a few yards nearer Norwich, it would have been on the bridge over the river and the loss of life would have been much greater. As it was, more than twenty people were killed – including both train drivers and their firemen – and around forty were injured.

Although the speeds were quite low by modern standards – reported in the *Norfolk News* as being around twenty miles per hour and in the *Norfolk Chronicle and Norwich Gazette* as a 'good speed' – the collision pushed the Yarmouth train almost vertical so that it landed on the top of the Norwich engine. The carriages were piled up to a height of fifteen or twenty feet, and then the train rolled over, taking the carriages with them. A piece of iron was hurled from the train and knocked a huge hole in the back of an outbuilding thirty yards from the line.

The trains were pretty evenly matched, weight for weight. Both trains were in two sections as they usually split at Reepham to cover the Lowestoft line.

The first section of the Norwich (down) train was the engine itself and the tender, driven by Thomas Clarke with fireman Frederick Sewell; both were killed. This was followed by a horsebox, which was smashed completely, and the mule inside it died. Then there was a second-class carriage, an open third-class carriage, a first-class carriage, another third-class carriage, two 'composite' carriages, two more third-class carriages and the brake-van. The smaller Lowestoft section was one second-class, one first-class and one third-class carriage, followed by the brake van

The first section of the Yarmouth mail train was the engine and tender, driven by John Prior with fireman James Light; again, both were killed. This was followed by a fish truck – which apparently absorbed some of the shock, though the cod inside slid all over the track – a brake van, two 'composite' carriages, a third-class carriage, the mail van and another 'composite' carriage. The smaller Lowestoft section was the brake van, a third-class carriage, a first-class carriage, two second-class carriages and a third-class carriage. Most of the Lowestoft passengers had been to the Lowestoft flower show that day. Although the carriages were packed, because the passengers were so far at the rear of the train, they sustained only a few minor cuts and bruises.

One of the passengers, John Devonshire from Lynn, said that he was 'thrown about the carriage in a very violent manner, bleeding a good deal from the nose and well nigh smothered with blood'. He was travelling with his brother Henry, a fish merchant, and Mr Winch, a fruiterer; they heard a cry of 'the mail train is coming' but they all thought they'd been derailed, not that the train had hit them head-on.

The noise of the crash was so loud that the residents of Thorpe rushed out to see what was going on, and one witness described the noise as 'sharp, like a thunderclap' followed by two thuds. Mr Sproul, the station master at Thorpe, sent cabs round to the doctors in the city and laid on a special train to take them to the crash site. The doctors at Thorpe Asylum also came to help and sent some sufferers to the hospital using the asylum van.

There were a couple of doctors already on the train. Dr Eade of Lowestoft had been knocked out of his carriage into the marsh, and he escaped with just a few minor cuts to his face. He was well enough to start helping the injured, but the surgeon Mr Bransby Francis, also on board, had been 'dangerously injured' with five broken ribs and a fractured thigh.

The doctors worked to set fractures and temporarily dress wounds, then sent the injured at intervals back to Norwich by the special train. Most of the dead bodies – with the exception of the leather merchant George Page and the clothier Mr Womack – were placed in the boat house of Mr Field, near the accident site, or in a room specially set aside at Thorpe Gardens. Some of the dead bodies were described as 'being without a whole bone'; they'd been crushed and mangled in the impact.

Amazingly, some of the uninjured passengers didn't even realise that there had been a crash, and they spoke of feeling a 'slight oscillation'. One drunken fisherman was found lying insensible across a seat and, when he woke, was shocked to find he'd slept through the entire incident. Another person who had been lying down escaped with bruises, whereas his fellow traveller sitting up at the end of the same seat was killed.

Some had an amazing escape. Horace Booty, master of the Presbyterian School in Calvert Street, objected to the rough conversation of a fellow traveller in their third-class carriage and moved his wife and family to another carriage. Their original carriage was smashed to pieces and, if they hadn't moved, they would all have died. Mr Mason, the Baptist minister at Attleborough, was chatting to friends when he felt a violent shaking, saw his friends disappear and was then carried over them out of the carriage, losing a boot in the process but at least keeping his life. Mrs Stevens and her children were sitting in the carriage next to the engine. When its bottom was knocked out, they escaped without hurt. One of the children fainted – when she came to, she found herself sitting on a pile of fish!

Mr Dimock of Fine Art Gallery said he felt a violent shock which knocked him across the carriage; the lights went out and the carriage collapsed. He crawled out of the train and burned his wrist on the hot funnel of the engine, and he didn't see anyone coming out for a while. Then he saw Mr England, Captain Oaks and Major Tunnsley climbing out of the topmost wrecked carriage with barely a scratch, to help rescue the injured, dying and dead.

Others weren't so lucky. Mr Womack changed places with a young lady who was travelling with a young child, on her request. They ended up with only minor injuries, but he was killed. Another passenger, Miss Woolasten, said it was like a sudden passing into darkness. All the lights went out and then Colour-Sergeant Ward and Sergeant-Major Cassell, who were sitting near her, went down through the bottom of the carriage. Both died. She was thrown out of the door and nearly all the clothes were torn from her body. She didn't even think she was injured, at first, but when she tried to sit up she discovered that her knee was fractured and her 'foot and leg reversed'.

Mr Richard White, a dentist from St Giles, was jammed in beneath a railway carriage for three and a half hours while the rescuers sawed through the wood and iron bar on top of him to make a hole large enough to get him out. He described his position later as 'like a man in a coffin bottom upwards' and he was in excruciating pain. To stop him fainting, Dr Pitt and others in the rescue team soaked a hanky in brandy, put it on the end of a stick and slid it up to his mouth so he could suck the liquor through the hanky.

The crash took place at night; the rescue operation, difficult enough in the dark, was hampered by torrential rain. The rescue teams lit huge bonfires on either sides of the crash to help them see what they were doing, and actually used bits of the wreck to fuel the flames, though the search for bodies ended at four in the morning. Local people – both rich and poor – gave up pillows and blankets to help sufferers, and tore sheets into strips to make bandages.

The death toll included John Prior, James Light, Thomas Clark and Frederick Sewell, the engine drivers and firemen; Sergeant-Major Cassell and Colour-Sergeant Ward of the West Norfolk Militia, both leaving a wife and family; Mrs Betts, the wife of the stoker in the Yarmouth train, and her 6-week-old child; Mr Page, a Norwich currier; Mr Womack, a Norwich clothier; the Revd Henry Stacey from Beccles and his wife; Mr Skinner, a 'gentleman' from Newmarket Road; Mrs Taylor, a forewoman from Caley's of Norwich; Miss Lincoln, an elderly servant; Miss Murray; Mrs Gilding and her 4-year-old daughter; Mr Skinner; and a 30-year-old man who was later identified as Mr Slade, through a shirt and a letter in his luggage at a Yarmouth hotel when he didn't return from his Norwich trip.

John Betts, the Yarmouth train stoker, died in hospital five days later from skull and brain injuries, leaving an orphaned 3-year-old son, Charles, who'd merely sustained a scalp wound. Susan Brown, who had been diagnosed with a dislocated ankle, turned out to have severe internal injuries and died on 15 September from injuries to the liver. Of the others taken to hospital, there were two more 'dangerous' cases: William Stowers, who had severe leg injuries and fractured ribs, and John Beart, whose smashed arm was amputated and the hospital bulletin said he was 'doing better' after that. Other injuries from the hospitalised cases included two fractured skulls, five people suffering from contusions, four cases of scalp wounds, one sprained knee, nine cases with fractured legs, and another case of fractured ribs.

Those who weren't hospitalised included four cases of cut faces, five cases of leg injuries, twenty cases of contusions (including 6-year-old Helen Squire and John Bartram, who also lost a front tooth), one case of 'damage to head', one case of broken ribs plus a broken thigh, one injured shoulder, and five other unspecified cases of injury. A 19-year-old, Miss Ramsgate, had her foot taken off; horribly, the surgeons had to amputate twice.

The *Standard* remarked how strange it was that an accident should happen so near to the headquarters of one of the largest insurance companies. Meanwhile, the Railway Passengers Assurance Company panicked and sent someone down from London to assess the injuries. To their relief, very few people had taken out an insurance ticket from the company, and the only one of their policyholders who was injured had fractured ribs and a sprained ankle.

The hospital had to work overtime to deal with all the patients. T. W. Crosse, surgeon at the Norfolk and Norwich Hospital, sent a terse bulletin at 9 p.m. on 12 September: 'Much trouble and inconvenience have been occasioned at the Hospital by numerous inquiries and visits that are made by friends and acquaintances of the inmates, which not only entail great additional labour upon the executive, but are also calculated to prejudice the recovery of the patients.' Presumably this embarrassed the visitors into staying at home because a bulletin two days later pointed out that: 'The Hospital has been much quieter today and a consequent improvement has taken place in many of the sufferers.'

The funerals of the dead were another cause of distress. While the engine driver Thomas Clarke was being buried in the Mortuary Chapel, a train whizzed by; newspaper reports say that his wife 'became hysterical and needed to be removed from the building'.

So who was to blame for the accident? Mr J. Hadfield, the secretary to Great Eastern, blamed the night inspector. The Board of Trade enquiry took testimonies to find out the truth. William Platford, who had been the station master at Brundall for over eight years, testified that between eighteen and twenty trains passed up and down each way daily. According to him, Brundall was a 'meeting station' because the line was double from Reedham to Brundall and single from Brundall to Norwich, and there was a mail train every day that met the express at Brundall, plus an excursion train on Mondays. His job was to detain the mail train from Yarmouth until the express arrived from Norwich, unless he had instructions to do otherwise. The exception was when the train was late from Norwich, and the mail train was sent on. It didn't happen often; twice in September, five times in August, seven times in July and not at all in June.

Importantly, there was a routine that had to be followed. The station master was obliged to write the telegram down and enter it in a book; he then had to put the instructions in writing and give them to the guard, who then gave them to the driver.

On the night of the collision, Platford claimed he received a telegram at 9.26: 'Send up mail train on to Norwich before the 9.10 p.m. down passenger train leaves. A. Cooper.' He replied immediately: 'I will send the up mail train on to Norwich before 9.10 p.m. down train leaves Norwich.' At 9.38, he got another, unsigned, telegraph from Norwich, this time saying 'stop mail train'; but once the train had left he couldn't recall it. He immediately replied 'Brundall up mail train left'. He admitted that he was anxious to get the train going so he'd broken his usual rule and, instead of giving the guard written instructions, he told the driver verbally, then informed both guards on the train.

The evidence from Thorpe station at Norwich slightly contradicted these details. John Robson had been the telegraphic clerk at Thorpe Station for fourteen years and told the court that the telegraph booth at the station was a public one, connected with the post office. They weren't allowed to take messages verbally or send unsigned messages; anyone in the office who was free would write down the telegraph message, put it on the instrument and then the clerk would enter it. But on the night of 10 September he had a verbal message from the night inspector Alfred Cooper, in the presence of John Keeble (a goods clerk) and three others, to send the mail train to Norwich. Robson wrote it down and didn't bother getting a signature; the entry in the book at 9.24 was 'send up mail train on to Norwich before the 9.10 p.m. down passenger train leaves Norwich.' He took the reply at 9.24: 'I will send the up mail train on to Norwich before the 9.10 p.m. down passenger train leaves Norwich – W. Platford.' The book was then put on one side for the inspector to see at 9.32 – when Cooper came in 'in a state of agitation and great excitement' and told Robson to cancel the message and stop the mail train. Robson telegraphed Brundall and said, 'stop mail' but Brundall replied 'mail left'. Robson knew that an accident was inevitable and sent for the day clerk and the clerk in charge. But Cooper refused to sign the original message and said that he hadn't given Robson any message.

Cooper's story was that on Thursday 10 September, the express train from London came in at 9.23 p.m., twenty-three minutes late. It was his duty to order up the mail, and if the London train was twenty-five minutes late the custom was to get the mail train from Yarmouth. Cooper went to the wicket at 9.21 and ordered the mail up; Robson was to write the telegram (which Cooper said he usually signed later). Then he saw the express train pull into the station and told Robson, 'Don't order the mail up.' He saw that Robson hadn't written the order in the telegraph book, and Robson said, 'All right, Captain' – his usual nickname for Cooper. Inspector Parker asked Cooper if he'd ordered the mail train; Cooper said no, so Parker told him to get the express train off and gave the express 'right away' at 9.30. Cooper then went to advise Robson of the starting time for the Reedham train and Robson said, 'I've ordered the mail.' Cooper asked why Robson had done it when he'd been told not to do so, but Robson claimed he hadn't heard Cooper's order.

Hayden, the ticket inspector, came up and asked what the

matter was. Cooper told him that the mail train was already on its way. Sproule, the station master, heard raised voices and the word 'mail' and rushed out of his office to find out what was going on. Cooper, white as chalk, told him the awful truth.

At the inquest, James Robertson, Superintendent of the Great Eastern Railway line, said, 'Any telegraph clerk is to blame for sending a message before it is signed. He acts contrary to the instructions given to him by the telegraphic department . . . when a reply . . . is received, the signer should also sign it before it is acted upon.' Robson had sent the message without a signature, and he hadn't called Cooper back to sign it when Cooper failed to return. Robson claimed he didn't like to use the bell in the telegraph office to summon the inspectors because it made them angry.

On 3 October 1874, the city coroner recorded a verdict of manslaughter against Cooper and Robson; he said that as the line worked as an imperfect system, 'both may be proved to have been free from actual moral culpability'. Whatever the truth about whether Cooper rescinded his order and Robson heard him do so or just gave a polite reply – as there were four other people chatting to him in the telegraph office at the time – the result was a fatal collision. And although the wreckage of the mail train's engine showed that its regulator was shut and the tender brake was screwed down hard, in a desperate attempt to stop the train, it was hopeless. With visibility in the rain being reduced to about three hundred yards, and the slight curve of the rails, the trains never stood a chance.

8

THE GREAT FLOOD

The summer of 1912 was the wettest, dullest and the coldest of the century, and there was even frost on 3 August! But what happened at the end of August was unexpected. Rain had upset the harvest in August. Friday 23 and Saturday 24 of August were rainy, Sunday 25 showed a bit of improvement, but at 3 a.m. on Monday 26 August rain began in earnest. The rain lasted for thirty hours and was measured at 7.34 inches; the resulting floods were the worst on record caused by rain. Norwich was cut off for two days – train, cars, phones and telegraphs all failed. The floods swamped 750 acres and 3,600 buildings, including 35 churches and 60 factories. No less than 15,000 people were made temporarily homeless, 3 people were killed and 42 bridges were destroyed. The total damage was estimated at £100,000.

The rains caused subsidence all over the city; a hole in the road to Brundall was estimated at being able to hold two horses and carts. An enormous hole developed in Unthank Road and a gardener at the Catholic rectory noticed a hole at one end of the garden which was eighteen feet across, fifteen feet wide and six feet deep. The Unthank Road Baptist Church school hall, next door, was known to be built over a chalk pit, and the hole stretched for six feet under the side walls of the school hall. Something similar was found on Kett's Hill, though the newspapers of the day described it as a 'sand pocket' – the pavement outside the Ostrich pub on Kett's Hill collapsed, leaving a hole the width of a house and three feet deep.

The trams were brought to a standstill on Unthank Road. The train lines from Norwich to Lowestoft and Norwich to Ipswich were damaged, and there were boats in the street in St Martin's.

Peacock Street stood twenty inches deep in water, the day after the floods, and two 100-feet-tall beech trees fell down. The rain came down so hard that soil was washed off the castle mound and dumped in Opie Street and Davey Place, and the basement of Curl's department store (then in the market place) was flooded. The waters rose so quickly around Martineau Lane that several pigs in the area drowned. The bridge over the Yare collapsed and the water ran through it 'at cataract speed'. The road at the mill at Cringleford was described as a torrent of foaming water.

Industry was affected too. Read's mills in Heigham were flooded to a depth of four and a half feet, Bullard's malthouse collapsed and the whole front of the *Norwich Mercury* offices was torn away and its boiler carried away by the river. Colman's was brought to a standstill at Carrow when the rain caused a landslide at Carrow Abbey; the electrical station was under water, leaving the site in darkness, and the third starch cellar-floor was under more than three feet of water. As soon as the water seeped into the bottom of a pile of starch, it quickly spread up the pile and ruined it completely – so the salvage operations required 'extraordinary methods'. According to contemporary reports, 'naked men were a common sight on Tuesday' – holes were bored into the basement floors and starch handed up to a chain of workers by lamplight, and even so 650 tons of starch were ruined.

Surprisingly, only three people died; but one species of Norwich canary was lost. Contemporary reports described the rain as a 'downpour and half a gale of wind'. It was impossible for traffic to move in the streets and some of the roads were flooded quickly.

Between 9 a.m. and 1 p.m. two and a half inches of rain fell, almost as much as the previous record of two and a quarter inches in twenty-four hours! And it didn't let up, as close to two more inches of rain fell in the next hour. At 3 p.m., the rain was described as a 'blizzard'; it was raining so hard that it looked like clouds of smoke in the street. The Heigham and Coslany areas were the worst hit, and by 6 a.m. the streets there were already filled with water.

Some people were determined to beat the rain. The taxi-driver

Spaul of Castle Hill was asked to take some 'well-known Norwich gentlemen' to Wroxham. What should have taken forty minutes there and back took seven hours. When they got to the Blue Boar at Sprowston, they were confronted with a small lake. Spaul and another car decided to brave the elements, but the water was two feet deep and they were both stuck in the middle. A horse and cart pulled both cars out, but Mr Spaul didn't learn his lesson; when he came to another lake near the Green Man at Rackheath, he got stuck again and the water got into the ignition. The passengers went for a drink while Spaul tried to get the engine to work and, when it finally fired, their road was blocked by a tree. He tried the back roads and the passengers had to help pull the car from the water. They ended up at Coltishall, where the road was dry; Spaul dropped his passengers off, but when he tried driving back along the same road, he found it under thirty inches of water. Three men had to pull him out, and then he ran into a fallen tree, three miles outside Norwich. By the time he got home, he was covered in bruises and his car was considerably damaged.

The river burst its banks at Thorpe, and people could only just get under the railway bridge in a small boat. But the rain also inspired heroic rescues. Just before midnight on the Tuesday, Norwich police officers rescued four children – aged from just four months to nine years – from a house in Hansard's Lane, Fishergate; their parents were frantic because they were unable to reach the children.

Volunteers from Norwich YMCA manned rowing boats to rescue people in Heigham, sailing through badly flooded streets where people were calling for help from their bedroom windows, and distress calls from women and children moved the rescuers to tears. One of the boats capsized and dumped the rescued people in ten feet of water. Another volunteer had a narrow escape when the ladder gave way, but luckily it crashed into the window frame downstairs, saving him and the blind 84-year-old woman he'd rescued from a ducking.

A small boy had a narrow escape. He was on his own in a cottage in Orchard Street, when a policeman and a volunteer rowed over to rescue him. The policeman leaned his hands on the windowsill and kept the boat steady with his feet, and directed the boy to crawl over his back into the boat. But the extra weight capsized the boat, throwing the three of them into the freezing cold and fast-running river. The policeman grabbed hold of the boy and they stood on the top step of the cottage to keep their heads above the water until the next boat came along.

Several babies were born in the floods. One man ran in anguish from the Flower-in-Hand Yard in Heigham, distraught because his wife was in labour. How could the midwives possibly get through the flooded streets, particularly as it was almost too dark to see? Councillor Louis Tillett and a policeman came to the rescue; Tillett found two nurses and he and the policeman carried them through Cushion's timber yard and waded for fifty yards through five feet of water, carrying the nurses on their shoulder and managing to scale two brick walls. They got the nurses in through a ladder to the bedroom window and the baby was born safely; though Tillett ripped his hand on wire in the garden so badly that it had to be surgically repaired. His excuse for missing the council meeting, the next morning, was simply that he'd 'hurt his hand'.

Though another rescue ended in tragedy. George Brodie, a fish porter from Oak Street, took a huge part in the rescue operations, despite suffering from asthma. Together with Herbert Nixon of Saw Mill Yard, he waded through water four feet deep from 6.45 p.m. to 11.30 p.m., carrying women and children through the thirty miles-per-hour current to the Corporation carts and safety.

Every half an hour or so, he returned to his wife, Annie Elizabeth Brodie, to check that she was all right. When he came back at 9 p.m., Annie was concerned about him; she thought the 46-year-old was already tired and should stay home and rest. George's reply was an emphatic shake of the head: 'There are some more dear children to get out, and I shall not be long before I get home.' He gave Annie his jacket – she told the coroner he appeared quite sober – and went back to his rescue work.

Nixon could hardly hold his footing; several times he called out to his friend, 'George, are you there?' Every time, Brodie called back cheerfully – until around 11.30 p.m., when he lost his footing and fell into the roaring torrent. Nixon had thought his friend was safe but then, the next morning, when he discovered that Brodie hadn't returned, Nixon went into the city to ask if anyone had seen him. On King Street, he had his answer when the ambulance came down bearing a body.

It was Brodie.

Frederick Fisher, aged 15, of Oak Street was wading near Bullard's with a friend at 10 a.m. the next morning when they found a body; they secured it and called for help. Shoe-finisher Thomas Shorten had been working in the floods for sixteen hours when he heard the cry for help; he rowed over, helped to drag the body into the boat and called the police. Brodie's hands were crossed over his chest, as if he'd had a heart attack; Nixon told the coroner that his friend must have become exhausted and been swept away by the current.

The other rescue that ended in tragedy was that of the Poll family. Ernest Charles Poll was coming home to Canterbury Place in Heigham Street at 8 p.m. when he saw that water was up to the bedroom windows. Indeed it was more like a millstream than the street he was used to. His wife Florence and two small children were upstairs, calling for help, so Ernest borrowed a small boat and sailed it to rescue his wife and the two children: a 2-year-old and a baby only 5 months old. Florence handed the children out of the window to Ernest, and then got into the boat.

But the current was strong and the boat struck some iron palings on Orchard Street and sank. Poll managed to grab his wife round the waist; she had one child held tightly under each arm. The water was as high as the front doors, and Poll swam to an empty house. Florence was unconscious. Poll shook her awake and grabbed hold of the 2-year-old. He asked Florence where the baby was – Florence, in horror, said that she must have let the baby go. Then Poll realised that baby Edward had been swept away by the floods; in the torrent, he stood almost no chance. By this time it was pitch dark and Poll didn't dare to leave his wife, for fear that she and their older child would drown too; he clung to his family and the boards from a window, and shouted for help. For ten long minutes, which seemed more like hours, they waited and, at last, the boat came and took Florence and her child to safety. They were taken by cart to a chapel on Dereham Road, then to her mother's house in Ashbourne Street. The boat came back later for Poll.

But it was too late for baby Edward, whose body was found in Brett's Yard at Heigham Street, the following day, his clothes caught on a nail. A gardener at Canterbury Place saw the baby's body go past on the current, but he couldn't do anything to help as he was stuck in an upstairs room. Mr Scarlett, the owner of the boat, said he'd only left the boat for a couple of minutes while he went home to change out of his wet clothes; he hadn't been asked to stand by the boat but he was anxious about it. At this, one of the jurors remarked tartly, 'I'd take any boat that was handy if I was going to save lives – I wouldn't ask questions!' The verdict was accidental death; the foreman of the jury said that, in view of the flood, it was 'an extraordinary thing' that they didn't have inquests into more deaths. The third fatality was a Mrs Kemp of Goat Yard, Oak Street, who was said to have died of 'fright and shock'.

An emergency council meeting was held on the Wednesday and a national flood relief was launched. A total of £24,000 was raised, including £150 from the King and Queen, £50 from the Prince of Wales and even the money collected for their annual summer treat by the Railway Mission Sunday School in Melton Constable because they felt the flood victims needed it more.

And although Norwich has been battered by gales and rain since, the flood of 1912 will live on in the collective memory as one of the worst ever to hit the city.

9

NORWICH IN THE BLITZ

During the Second World War, Norwich was very badly affected by enemy bombing. Out of the city's 35,000 houses, fewer than 5,000 sustained no damage, while 2,000 were completely destroyed and 2,600 seriously damaged.

Before the war, 126,000 gas masks were distributed (one for every person in the city); there were eleven warning sirens to send people down to the public shelters (which only had room for 122,000 people). The Women's Voluntary Service had 13 centres based at Norwich schools and could handle 2,000 cases of injuries, and there were 70 wardens around the city who had phone links to the rescue-party depots, ambulance depots and first-aid posts.

If the phone lines were out, the wardens used cyclists to deliver their messages; one of them, John Grix, showed real Norwich spirit. Although he was only 15 years old, he lied about his age so he could join the ARP service. He rode round the city on his bike during the Blitz, delivering messages; and although he was blown off his bike several times and burned by acid in a factory fire, he carried on. Perhaps not surprisingly he was awarded the British Empire Medal for bravery and devotion to duty.

Important buildings such as the Guildhall were sandbagged and Norwich thought it was prepared. On the first day of war, the alarm sounded but it was a false alarm, and in fact Norwich was safe from attacks for the first ten months of the conflict. But over the course of the war there were 1,443 alerts, or an average of one a day, and Norwich was raided forty-six times.

In 1940, 60 people were killed and 190 injured. The first raid on Norwich was on 9 July. Incendiary bombs set fire to a warehouse on Salhouse Road and high-explosive bombs fell on the Boulton & Paul riverside factory, leaving ten dead and seventy injured. More fell on Carrow Hill; no air raid warning was given and the attack came just as the Colman's factory workers were leaving for the day. The result was that twenty-six women were killed. Ten days later, there was another raid by a single aeroplane, damaging houses in the Magdalen Street area and killing one. A single aeroplane attacked the city at the end of the month, again with no air raid warning, and several houses collapsed and killed their occupants.

On 1 August 1940, another single plane bombed Norwich, this time setting fire to Boulton & Paul's joinery and following up by machine-gunning the streets. For the first time in the war (with the exception of the air raid on Dover Harbour), the press announced the name of the town that had been raided: Norwich. The following day, members of Norwich City Council met the Ministry of Home Security in London to discuss the air raid warning system.

There were two more raids in August, causing little damage. On 19 September, a 250-kilogram delayed-action bomb fell in Theatre Street and embedded itself into the path, and a large area of the city was evacuated for five days while the bomb was dug out by the disposal squad. There was another minor raid in October and two in November, without much damage. December saw three raids which killed several people, demolished three houses and fractured the water and gas mains in Mile Cross.

The next year, 1941, saw more damage to houses but fewer casualties; twenty people were killed and just over a hundred were injured. Most of the raids were at night and only two were in daylight.

The first raid of 1941 was on 5 January, by a single bomber. The bombs landed harmlessly on the golf course at Eaton and on the City of Norwich School playing fields. The bomber then flew over Unthank Road and machine-gunned the street, but the damage was minimal; just broken windows and tiles.

The three raids in February saw more casualties – two killed and several injured in the first attack on Boulton & Paul's and Plumstead Road, another eight killed when a whistling bomb landed on Vauxhall Street and flattened houses and shops, and yet more damage at Barnard's factory on Salhouse Road. March saw some lucky escapes; the bomb that fell on the roof of St Swithin's church melted the lead but was put out before it set light to the roof timbers. April saw Colman's being targeted again; several mills were burned out, seven people were hurt and one was killed. The firefighters were hindered by the fractured water-main, blocked roads and a building falling into the river where they would have got water. May saw more casualties and more deaths, including the mother, father and three of their six children on the Larkman Lane estate. Two more bombing raids on Dereham Road and Eaton caused little damage – the eight bombs at Eaton didn't even explode – and then Norwich had plenty of air raid warnings but no more raids for several months.

But all that changed with the Baedeker raids in 1942, so called because the Luftwaffe High Command decided to hit the places in Britain that were marked in *Baedeker's* guide as having great historical significance. The Baedeker raids were a reprisal for the assassination of Heydrich, Himmler's deputy, in Czechoslovakia. Norwich was one of the cities 'starred' in Baedeker. And the Baedeker raids had a deadly effect; they caused 60 per cent of Norwich deaths through air raids during the war.

After the lull in bombing, Norwich was at the point where people had actually started to ignore the air raid sirens. But on Monday 27 April 1942, on a bright moonlit night at twenty past eleven, the sirens sounded. People paid no attention, thinking it was another false alarm. Twenty minutes later, a bomber flew over the city and dropped incendiaries on the city station in Heigham. The felted wooden roofs and timber posts went up in flames. Five minutes later, the main attack started. One or two aircraft at a time circled the city, avoiding anti-aircraft fire with ease, then dived down and bombed their targets. In all, between twenty-five and thirty planes bombed the city. The city was lit with parachute flares and soon it was on fire, the orange glow visible for miles as Norwich burned.

Over the course of two hours, the Luftwaffe dropped 185

bombs weighing a total of more than 50 tons. Streets were flattened, particularly in the Heigham area. The city station was burned to a shell and the locomotive shed and passenger coaches were gutted, as was the goods depot.

It's possible that the first bomber – which dropped the 'marker' bomb – targeted the wrong station, as most of the factories were close to Thorpe Station rather than the city station. So the main attack turned out to be in a residential area rather than an industrial zone. A total of 600 people were injured and 162 were killed; many were buried under debris, though the rescue services managed to dig out 84 people, tunnelling through the debris.

People took shelter where they could; in Miller's Lane, an Anderson shelter designed to hold six people protected nine adults and two children. A nearby bomb threw debris into the shelter, but all bar one came out alive.

The water mains were smashed, hindering attempts to put out the flames. Five units from neighbouring towns came to help the Norwich firefighters; the fire depot at Westwick was flattened and all the firewatchers there were killed.

More than 14,000 emergency ration cards were issued the next day but people couldn't get more clothes because the shops had been wiped out. Somehow, the castle, cathedral, Guildhall and City Hall were still standing; the bombers had missed the most important buildings in Norwich. Contemporary accounts of the Nazi version of events state that 'bomber formations last night carried out a reprisal attack against the town of Norwich' and that 'numerous high explosive and incendiary bombs were dropped on the town'.

On Tuesday night, the German bombers concentrated on York. But the people of Norwich lived in fear; many women trudged out of the city at night with their tearful children, pushing their possessions in prams and barrows. After the first Baedeker raid, they felt it was safer to sleep in the fields around the city at night before returning in the morning.

They were right to be concerned. On the Wednesday night, the Luftwaffe were back in Norwich; the warning sirens sounded at quarter past eleven. Although the attack lasted roughly half the length of that on Monday night, it was more intense, as 112 high explosive bombs and incendiaries weighing a total of 45 tons landed on the city. Another sixty-nine people were killed and nearly ninety were badly injured. This time, the city was ready for the attack. When the alarms sounded, everyone went straight to the public shelters, or to their own Anderson or Morrison shelters.

The electricity and sewerage systems were hit. Most of the bombs were incendiaries so the city was on fire and, because the water mains had been hit on Monday, there were water shortages which hindered attempts to put the fires out. Bad hits included St Stephen's – the city lost the ancient thatched Boar's Head Inn on the corner of Surrey Street and St Stephen's. Curls (now Debenham's) and Bunting's (now Marks and Spencer's) were demolished. St Benedict's church was blown up and only the Norman round tower was left. Nelson Street school went up in flames, because the lone fire-watcher simply couldn't cope with the number of incendiary bombs. Bishop Hall's palace (the Dolphin Inn) went up in flames, as did Barker's Engineering Works. The Clarks shoe factory was hit by incendiary bombs – and the strong wind sent the flames straight to the wooden lasts and leather stocks. The fire watchers couldn't cope with the flames, and the lines were down so they were unable to call the fire service. By the time firefighters did arrive, an hour and a half later, the factory was gutted. St Mary's Silk Mills suffered the same fate.

The Mackintosh chocolate factory (still known locally as Caley's) had their own fire brigade. When the printing works next door went up in flames, Caley's tried to help. The water pressure of the mains was too low, so they tried using their own supplies – their well filled up the supply tanks on the factory roof. But they couldn't stop the printing works being gutted and, because their fire brigade's pump used three times as much water per hour than their supply tanks could produce, there wasn't enough water for Caley's to save their own factory when the windows shattered under the blast of a high-explosive bomb and the burning debris set all the factory floors alight at the same time. The fire ripped through 1,000 tons of chocolates and the packaging, and the two six-storey buildings were gutted.

The Hippodrome was also bombed; the blast killed the stage manager, his wife and the trainer of a troupe of performing sea lions. The sea lions were released by the bombs and one apparently flapped through the theatre, wailing for his master. Buddy, known as 'the world's greatest comedy seal', died soon after; probably from a broken heart.

The bombing stopped at midnight, but the city burned for hours afterwards. And the Nazis were satisfied at their 'reprisal for the raid on Kiel'; they felt that 'good results were obtained'.

May Day saw another attack, concentrated on Heigham Street, Duke Street and St Andrew's Street. Barnard's wire-netting works was hit and the fire closed down the works for the next ten days. Later in the month, the Duke of Kent visited the city and later wrote to J. H. Barnes, the Lord Mayor, saying how sorry he was about the damage to the city but also how impressed he'd been by the courage of the people.

On 27 June 1942, there was a raid on the cathedral, where bombers dropped around 850 incendiaries. Reginald Pallent and his team of firefighters stopped the cathedral burning down and only some of the lead on the roof melted, on the north and south transepts. Two houses in the close were destroyed. The Norfolk and Norwich hospital was hit, including the nurses' home, the main operating theatre and four wards. Bonds department store was wrecked and Ber Street was badly hit, flattening the church of St Michael at Thorn. St Julian's church in King Street was blown up by a high-explosive bomb which left only the north wall and porch standing. Amazingly, only sixteen people were killed and fifteen seriously injured.

Another incendiary raid at the end of July damaged St Benedict's again. August raids wiped out Page the house furnisher's in St John Maddermarket, the Sexton shoe factory in St Mary's Plain and Hurrell's shoe factory in Magdalen Street. A morning raid in September terrified shoppers in Magdalen Street and hit a joinery works in St Martin at Palace and a factory at Fishergate – five were killed and several injured.

King George VI paid a surprise visit to the city on 12 October. He made a twenty-five-mile tour round twenty-eight streets in the worst-hit areas of the city and talked to local people. A week later, there was a double raid; first at 7.15 a.m. in Carrow and then in Pottergate and Westwick Street at 11 a.m. The city had a lucky escape in November, when bombs were dropped at the bus station, All Saints Green and the cattle market, but none of them exploded.

1943 saw a much lower level of activity. There were only five raids, which resulted in fourteen casualties and one death. The 'butterfly blitz' referred to the two-kilogram winged-bombs dropped from the planes, and 270 of them were made safe by the bomb-disposal team. On New Year's Day, North Heigham was bombed but there were no casualties. 18 March saw the worst raid of the year; F. W. Harmer's clothing factory on St Andrew's Street was burned to the ground, and two people there were seriously hurt. A raid on 5 May was again concentrated on St Andrew's, damaging the church and destroying a baker's shop, estate agency and restaurant. The railway was slightly damaged in the small raid of 7 October, and Unthank Road was hit on 6 November.

Through 1944 and 1945 no more bombs landed on Norwich. Forty-six 'Big Ben' bombs (otherwise known as V2s) were aimed at the city in September and October 1944, but luckily none were accurate; the nearest one landed on the golf course at Hellesdon. And 20,000 people were evacuated from London to Norwich during 3 days in July 1944.

The last siren sounded on 27 March 1945. The cost of repairs, according to the city engineers, was £1,060,000; £280,000 of this was for materials and haulage. The rebuilding statistics are impressive: 23,450 ceilings, 2,300 chimney stacks, 19,850 doors and window frames were repaired, and an incredible 610,000 feet of glass was used to replace shattered windows.

10

FIRE AND PESTILENCE

Norwich has had its fair share of fire, World War Two apart. One of the earliest recorded fires in the city was in 1413 when most of St Andrew's Hall was destroyed, though the hall was completely rebuilt by 1470.

The early sixteenth century was even worse, with severe fires in 1502 and 1505, and two in 1507. The first fire of 1507, in March, lasted for four days and over 700 houses were burned. Another 360 houses were lost in the second fire, in June, which lasted for two days. Almost half of the city's housing had been destroyed; the severity of the fire's effects shows in the rents from the tenements, which dropped from several pounds to only a few pence per year. The danger of fire led to a decision by the corporation that, from 1509 onwards, all new buildings should have a tiled roof and that no thatch was allowed. Anyone using thatch or 'reed straw' could be fined twenty shillings.

In 1570, another order warned about the danger of sparks being carried on the wind. Anyone who didn't use tile or lead on their roofs would be fined (unless a roof had to be repaired and there was a thatched house on either side) and the fine money would go towards paying for fire buckets and ladders. Every alderman had to have twelve buckets and a ladder in his house. The signal for fire would be a backwards peal of bells and, as soon as a carrier or brewer heard it, they had to carry buckets of water straight to the fire.

There are only five thatched houses left now within the city walls: a house in Hampshire Hog Yard (which used to be the Hampshire Hog pub; its landlord, John 'Licker' Pratt, beat Jem Mace in a bare-knuckle fight that lasted two hours in 1850);

Pykerell's House in Rosemary Lane (home of thrice-mayor Thomas Pykerell and at one point the Rosemary Tavern); the Briton's Arms on Elm Hill (which was the only building in Elm Hill to survive the 1507 fires); the Hermitage on Bishopsgate; and the 'Barking Dickey' on Westlegate (currently a coffee-house, Carsaccio's – its name comes from its previous incarnation as the Light Horseman pub, when the horse painted on the pub sign apparently looked more like a cross between a dog and a donkey or 'dickey'). Another thatched building – the Boar's Head on the corner of St Stephen's Street and Surrey Street – was a casualty of the Baedeker raids in World War Two.

1898 saw what the *Eastern Evening News* called 'an irreparable loss' when the subscription library was burned down in a fire that caused an estimated £100,000 of damage (most of it insured just a couple of streets away, at Norwich Union) and saw the largest number of firemen working together in the city on a blaze that took six hours to subdue. Outside Cambridge, the subscription library was the biggest library of its time in East Anglia. The library began in the porch of St Andrew's Hall, grew to take over the Chapel of the Duke of Norfolk in St Andrew's Street, and then in 1784 a new building was opened on Guildhall Hill. But it was gutted completely on 1 August 1898, when fire broke out at the ropemaker Daniel Hurn's. Mr and Mrs Booth, who lived around the corner in London Street, were walking through the area at 4 a.m. when they smelled burning and saw tar running down the gutters. Realising that something was wrong, they raised the alarm. The city fire-brigade were on the spot within minutes but, by half-past four, the fire had spread to Self the gas-fitter's shop, and to the cloth department at Chamberlin's. Mr Hurn and his assistants were helped from the house and Daniel Hurn was so shocked that he had to be carried out.

The servants and assistants sleeping at Chamberlin's took their personal belongings to the Guildhall for safety. The Carrow and Anchor Brewery fire brigades were in place by half-past six, but at seven the library caught fire. Mr Quinton, the secretary of the library, asked the firemen to put ladders up to the roof, but they didn't have any long enough, and the library ladders were too short. The flames took hold and in three-quarters of an hour all 60,000 volumes were lost. The roof caved in and the galleries collapsed. The ropemaker's shop collapsed wall by wall, and if the wind had been blowing in the opposite direction the whole of Dove Street and Lower Goat Lane would also have burned down. Luckily the fire didn't quite reach Mr Bagley's furniture workshop in Pottergate, which was well stocked with seasoned timber and would have gone up in seconds.

The cost of the damage at Chamberlin's alone was estimated at £80,000. And the secretary of the library, Mr Quinton, said that if ladders had been available the library could have been saved. Ironically, just before the fire broke out, the library catalogue had been finished and was about to go to the printer's. But thousands of rare books were reduced to ashes – and it was to happen again, less than a century later.

The next major fire in the city was on the other side of the market place, in Theatre Street, an area that would be hit twice more by fire in the twentieth century, not including the Second World War. On Friday 22 June 1934 the Theatre Royal – built 108 years earlier – was gutted. Contemporary sources described it as 'one of the fiercest fires ever seen in the city' and when reporters walked in to the back of the circle to gain a clearer picture of what was happening to the stage, they could only bear the heat and smoke for a couple of seconds.

Miss Bardwell, the assistant cashier, was on duty in the box office and heard a noise in the theatre at around eight minutes to two. She thought at first it was the stage manager, but when the noises continued she went to investigate. She saw flames licking under the safety curtain of the stage and rushed out into the street, shouting for help. The fire brigade was summoned and, although they worked flat out, a strong wind stopped them putting out the fire. The theatre acted as a kind of wind tunnel and the half-gale meant that the fire ripped through the building, gutting it in less than two hours. All the firemen could do was to protect adjoining property and, fortunately, the Assembly House was saved.

Most of the people working at the theatre that week lost their belongings. Scenery was destroyed and the band's instruments were burned, along with two grand pianos, a dulcimer and several drums. The contents of the dressing rooms escaped the fire but were damaged by water. Jack Gladwin, the owner, had several theatres around the country but said that 'the old Theatre Royal at Norwich was my pet' and the one he'd least wanted to lose. But the theatre was rebuilt and reopened on 30 September 1935 with the popular musical comedy, *White Horse Inn*.

Norwich suffered severe fire damage through the Blitz in 1942 (see chapter nine) but things seemed calmer until 1 August 1970, when Garlands' department store on the corner of London Street burned down. It started with a chip-pan fire in the restaurant, which then ripped through the cooking ducts and took hold of the first and second floors, turning what was at first a minor incident into a million-pound blaze, with the shop front collapsing completely. The alarm was sounded at 5 p.m. and nearly seventy firemen worked for three hours to stop the whole of London Street being gutted. The smoke was visible five miles away from the city.

Buckingham's shoe shop was also affected; a human chain passed hundreds of shoes into London Street to save them and within forty-five minutes the shop was stripped, right down to the curtains in the window. The rescue team could feel the wall of the shop adjoining Garlands getting hotter and hotter as they worked! By quarter to nine, the worst of the blaze was over and the damping-down started, though at twenty past midnight the hundred or so spectators could still see spasmodic flames.

The next big fire was again on 1 August – this time in 1994, when the library was burned down. It was the worst library fire in Britain since the war and thousands of books and archive material were lost in the 1,000-degree heat. The alarm was raised at 7.31 a.m.; three fire engines were sent straight away, followed by another three just three minutes later. Two more engines followed at 7.40 a.m. and Anglian

Water was asked to increase the pressure on the mains to give the firefighters more water. By 8.05 a.m. there were ten fire engines at the scene, with another five added within the next half hour.

Salvage started at ten, and most of the flames were out by noon. But the damage was done – two-thirds of the Colman collection and countless rare archive material was destroyed. Malcolm Bradbury commented that he was sick to his stomach and couldn't 'think of any other building . . . that I would feel more terrible about its burning down'.

A temporary library opened in Ber Street on 14 February 1995 and while the wrangle went on about what sort of building would replace the library (including the ill-fated 'Technopolis'), the city's archaeologists excavated the heart of the old French borough beneath the library, and discovered the only Viking gold ingot in Britain – a thin strip approximately twice the width of a 20p piece. Eventually agreement for the building of the Forum went ahead. The foundations were laid in June 1999 and the new library, housed in the Forum, finally opened in November 2001. The *Eastern Daily Press* held a poll about which book should be the first one back on the shelves; readers voted for Thomas Paine's *Rights of Man*, the first of 120,000 books on the seven miles of shelving. (Though this book was once regarded as extremely dangerous; it was instrumental in a nineteenth-century murder case, described in chapter fourteen.)

The Forum was officially opened by the Queen on 18 July 2002 during her Jubilee visit to the city, where she sent an e-mail message to over 114,000 children at 452 schools in Norfolk, the largest group e-mail she'd ever sent.

But only eight months after the library fire, flames again ripped through Norwich's heritage. On 12 April 1995, the Assembly House caught fire. The roof had only been refurbished five months previously in a £250,000 programme. The alarm sounded at the tearooms and more than one hundred firemen helped fight the blaze. Timothy Colman, the Lord Lieutenant of Norfolk, said, 'We have lost a priceless and much loved piece of our heritage.' And historic buildings consultant Dr Bill Watson added to the gloom when he said that the roof was 'probably irreplaceable'. But the kind of Norwich spirit that got us through the Blitz came to the fore again, and the Assembly House was reopened on 13 February 1997.

Fire isn't the only thing that has devastated Norwich. As one of the major cities in medieval and Renaissance Britain, Norwich was hit badly by the plague. Most of the epidemics in Norwich have been the result of the bubonic plague, an infectious fever caused by a bacilli transmitted by rat fleas. The disease got its name from the buboes or swollen lymph-nodes it caused in the groin and underarm areas, and was also known as the Black Death because the dried blood under the skin turned black. If you caught the plague, you had less than a 30 per cent chance of surviving.

In 1349, the Black Death (a mixture of bubonic and pneumonic plague) wiped out around a third of the population and half the clergy in Norwich. Church records show that Norwich, Exeter and Winchester were the worst-hit places in the country, and four churches in Norwich were closed because the whole congregation had died. According to the eighteenth-century historian Francis Blomefield, over 5,700 people died in Norwich between 1 January 1348 and 1 July 1349, 'besides religious and beggars'. 1361 saw another wave of plague, known as the 'second pestilence', followed by a third wave in 1369 which, according to Blomefield, 'seized the people so suddenly that many who went to bed well were found dead in the morning'.

Why was Norwich hit so badly? The way the city had grown up meant that cottages and tenements were crowded into the yards of the old merchant houses, back to back on narrow streets. The streets themselves were unpaved and never cleaned and, with no waste collection service, householders simply threw rubbish and dung straight from their houses into the streets. There was no system of street drainage, and the 'cockeys' or gulleys and streams that carried water down to the river were often blocked by rubbish and piles of earth. Water collected in hollows and became mud, mixed with refuse and dung from the pigs and hens allowed to wander round the streets. The mud washed into the cockeys and from there into the river Wensum, which became so polluted that the fish died out. The river water was useless for drinking; above the city it wasn't so bad, but below the city it was polluted by the work of the tanners, brewers and dyers. Most people got their water from the wells dotted around the city, and even these weren't particularly pure as they were very shallow.

People's diet was unhealthy, too. Vegetables were scarce. Rock salt wasn't discovered until 1670, so salt was expensive and people couldn't afford to salt meat properly to preserve it. When they ate meat, particularly in the winter, it had gone off and the taste of rotting meat was hidden by spices.

So with people crowded together in unsanitary conditions, their constitutions weakened anyway by a poor diet and bad water, infectious diseases spread rapidly. When the plague hit Norwich in 1349, people died so quickly that there wasn't time to bury them individually. Huge pits were dug in the churchyards and bodies thrown into them in heaps, lime poured over the top, and more bodies piled on top, so that the churchyards built up much higher than street level. By the end of the third wave of the plague, market stalls had fallen into ruin because there weren't enough people to sell the goods, or to buy them. Two rows of stalls were taken down and the land was added to St Peter Mancroft's churchyard, which badly needed it for burial purposes.

In August 1578 the plague hit again and wiped out nearly a third of the population. According to Blomefield, 2,335 English and 2,482 'alyan strangers' (Flemish weavers) died. The mayor stipulated that anyone from an infected house had to carry a small white wand two feet long in their hands and must not attend any courts, sermons or public places. He added that the clerk or sexton of every parish should set a paper on the door of every infected house, with the words 'Lord have mercy upon us' written on it, and it had to stay on the door until the house had been free from the infection for a whole month. And finally, if you had a plague sore, you weren't allowed to go into the city until you'd been clear of them for twenty days.

In 1602, the plague came again and wiped out around 3,000 people, although this was relatively light by comparison with London's loss, where nearly ten times as many people died. The plague caused food shortages in the city and wheat at the time was sold for ten shillings per bushel; rye was priced at six shillings and barley at five shillings. It had enough of an impact to be mentioned in the mayor's court records thirty years later; the weekly certificate from John Goodwyn for the city's christenings and burials actually stipulates 'but none of the plague' on most occasions (though there were minor outbreaks between 1631 and 1635).

October 1665 to October 1666 saw Norwich's last serious epidemic of bubonic plague, which originated in Yarmouth. According to Blomefield there were 2,251 deaths from plague in the period, and 203 died in just one month. 9 September 1667 was declared a public holiday when the plague was finally over. Though two years later, there was a different 'plague' in Norwich – smallpox, which caused the deaths of more than three hundred families in less than a fortnight.

In 1743, the *Norwich Gazette* published a recipe against the plague which apparently came from four men who'd robbed infected houses and murdered people during the plague. They confessed at the gallows that they'd saved themselves by using this medicine.

> Put a handful each of rue, sage, mint, rosemary, wormwood and lavender into a gallon of white wine vinegar in a covered stone pot, put the pot on warm wood ashes for eight days, then strain the liquid through fine flannel and add a quarter of an ounce of camphor to each quart bottle. Use this to wash your mouth and rub your loins and temples daily; snuff some of the mixture up your nostrils before you go into air; and dip a sponge into the mixture and carry it with you, so you can smell it when you're near an infected place or person.

The plague wasn't the only epidemic to sweep the city; there were cholera epidemics in Norwich in both 1831 and 1848. A government inspector made a detailed report in 1850 and described the water supply as 'bad in everything that should constitute a water supply'. Clearly not much had changed since the well system of the 1300s and the water piped through lead in the 1570s. At the time, Norwich had one of the highest death rates in the country, and children were among the most vulnerable; a quarter of deaths in 1873 were of children under 5. The city appointed a medical officer of health in 1875 and a new sewerage-system and slum-clearance programme began in the 1870s. The slum clearances changed the character of the city – but it also improved health to the point where the death rate in 1980 was half that of 1877, though the population was more than double.

11

HAUNTED NORWICH

For a city so steeped in history, Norwich has surprisingly few ghosts.

Though unsurprisingly, given the number of pubs in the city's history, several of the ghosts inhabit pubs. The Adam and Eve is the oldest pub in Norwich and is haunted by more than one ghost; one is thought to be Lord Sheffield, who was beheaded during Kett's rebellion by Fulke the butcher. Apparently, the beheading wasn't complete. Sheffield didn't die straight away, so his men carried him into the Adam and Eve and laid him on a table, where he died. Customers have claimed to feel a tap on the shoulder, but turned round to find no one behind them. Car keys left on a table have disappeared, only to reappear in exactly the same place a couple of days later. Tankards have been seen swinging over the bar when all the doors and windows are shut, and staff have heard banging on locked doors, although these may be the ghosts of the monks from the nearby cemetery.

The cellar of the nearby Bridge House was once used as a dungeon and it's believed that it was also the location of the Lollard's pit, where people were burned at the stake for heresy; though some sources say the pit was further to the right, under what is now the car park of Godfrey's DIY.

One of the martyrs burned in the Lollard's pit was Thomas Bilney. He was probably born in Norwich around 1495, though local tradition has it that 'Martyr's Cotttage' in East Bilney belonged to his parents and he was born there. He went to Corpus Christi College in Cambridge when he was around 14 years old, to study canon law, as he intended to enter church administration. In later life, he talked about his 'negligent and reckless life', but some unknown spiritual crisis led him to study religion seriously. He was troubled by guilt and spoke to many doctors about his problem; they all recommended 'fasting, watching, buying of pardons and masses', but Bilney found that fasting, prayers, penances and good works weren't enough to help him.

And then he went to a lecture by the Dutch scholar Desiderius Erasmus around 1511 and heard a reading of the New Testament. He was profoundly affected by it and even wrote: 'I chanced upon this sentence of St Paul (O most sweet and comfortable sentence to my soul) in I Timothy I – "It is a true saying, and worth of all men to be embraced that Christ Jesus came into the world to save sinners, of whom I am the chief and Principal." This one sentence . . . did so exhilarate my heart, being before wounded with the guilt of my sins, and being almost in despair, that immediately I felt a marvellous comfort and quietness insomuch "that my bruised bones leaped for joy".' (Psalm I i)

In 1514, he attended a sermon given by Hugh Latimer and sought him out afterwards, begging Latimer to hear his confession. What Latimer heard changed his thinking for good. 'By his confession I learned more than afore in many years. So from this time forward I began to smell the word of God and forsook the school doctors and all such fooleries.'

Bilney spent more time studying the scriptures than law, ate only one meal a day and took all his spare food to prisons and lazar houses. According to John Foxe in his *Book of Martyrs* (written a few years later in 1596), Bilney hated music and when the future Bishop of Norwich, Dr Thirlby, played his recorder, Bilney started praying! He rejected the worship of saints and attacked pilgrimages and miracles; he also said that the Pope should live a true Christian life. This was unpopular with the churches because pilgrimages and the worship of saints brought a lot of money into the church.

Bilney was ordained in 1519. During the 1520s his friends had trouble with the authorities. Dr Barnes was made to recant his heretical views, Latimer was banned from preaching, and Tyndale's 1526 translation of the New Testament into English was burned publicly. In 1527 Bilney had to appear before Cardinal Wolsey and was only allowed to continue preaching on condition that he didn't preach Lutheran doctrine. Then he went back to preach in East Anglia and was pulled out of the pulpit three times for heretical sermons! In 1527 he was put on a formal charge of heresy. After three refusals to recant and long discussions with his friends, he agreed to recant and perform public penance, carrying a bundle of sticks at Paul's Cross. He was kept in the Tower of London for over a year. In 1529 he was released but forbidden to preach. He was tortured by guilt and in 1531 decided to preach what he believed. He walked from Cambridge to Norwich, preaching all the way in fields and market places rather than churches.

In Norwich, he was arrested; he was found guilty of being a relapsed heretic and was condemned to be burned at the stake. He spent his last days in the cells beneath the Guildhall. Foxe said Bilney tested his courage by placing his finger in a candle-flame, then wrote a letter to his parents, saying he was 'as hale and merry as ever I was in my life'. Matthew Parker and William Warner heard his confession. And then on 19 August Bilney was taken to the Lollard's Pit. The Mayor gave him a formal 'abjuration' to read but apparently Bilney read it so quietly that no one heard it.

Bilney's last words to the crowd were, 'Good people, I am come hither to die. I depart out of this present life as a true Christian man in a right belief towards almighty God.' He said his prayers at the stake and the officers set light to the reeds and faggots round his body. The flames blew to and fro, then finally he 'gave up the ghost, and his body being withered bowed downward upon the chain'.

In the Tap and Spile (now the White Lion) in Oak Street, bottles and glasses have been moved and footsteps overhead – possibly those of a former landlord who was sent to the gallows for the murder of a prostitute.

In the Lamb, another former landlord is supposed to haunt the place – John Aggas, killed by his brother-in-law in November 1787. The trouble started when Aggas married; his wife's brother Timothy Hardy was easily led and got in with a bad crowd. Hardy and Aggas had several arguments and Aggas even threw his brother-in-law out. Hardy was furious at the public humiliation and decided to get even. So he treated his friends to a free drinking session at his brother-in-law's expense, and smuggled them in through the cellar flap. Aggas heard a noise in the cellar and came downstairs with a staff in his hand, ready to see off any burglars. The group dispersed, but then Hardy came up the stairs with a knife and stabbed Aggas. He was hanged, but Aggas's footsteps can still be heard on a quiet night.

Though once houses or pubs have been pulled down, it seems that the ghosts move on too. In January 1700, a drama took place in the Old Globe at St Augustine's which saw an innocent woman murdered. The weaver Robert Watts, who frequented the Globe, was a terribly jealous man and the patrons of the pub used to enjoy winding him up. One of them bet him that he could get Mrs Watts' wedding ring (presumably telling Watts that it would be for a sexual favour). Mrs Watts was clearly a trusting soul, because when her husband's friend came over to their house in nearby Botolph Street and asked to borrow her ring, claiming that Watts had made a bet about its weight, she gave it to him. He went straight to Watts, saying that it had been easy and he would recognise the ring from the inscription in it. Watts flew into a jealous rage, went home and cut his wife's throat. He was hanged at his own door in August 1700. The ghost of Mrs Watts was meant to haunt the house, but when the house was pulled down in 1875 no more was heard of the ghost.

Given the number of executions there, it's only to be expected that Norwich Castle should be haunted. There are two alleged ghosts there; one is a skull, the other a woman. The woman used to terrify prisoners in the cells and has been seen on occasion by staff at the castle. Some people have suggested that it's actually Martha Alden, the Bill-hook murderess (whose story is told in chapter fifteen).

There are no reports of ghosts at the cathedral – despite its somewhat turbulent history – but Tombland is a different matter. The old Samson and Hercules nightclub in Norwich was built over the site of a plague pit, and apparently monks have been seen in the building. In the days when it was a YWCA, people staying in a certain room had nightmares about being buried alive. There is also supposed to be a grey lady who haunts the place and the alleyway next to Augustine Steward's house; during the plague she was locked in the house and left to die.

On one night, well after the doors had closed and everyone had gone home, the staff at Central Park (formerly the Samson and Hercules) looked up and saw someone running past the windows upstairs. They thought maybe someone had been locked in by mistake: but when the security guards checked, there was nobody there; and the place was ice-cold.

One of the great city fires is responsible for another ghost, in the Stranger's Club in Elm Hill. A family burned to death in the fire of 1507; although the house was burned to the ground and a new house was built on the spot, apparently people often hear footsteps on the first floor – when there's nobody there.

The most haunted place in the city is reputed to be 19 Magdalen Street, haunted by the ghost of a woman murdered in Victorian times. Pieces of paper floated across the room, cups fell from desks when no one was near them, typewriters worked themselves, people felt a presence in the place and there were unexplained cold spots in the shop. Others claimed to hear footsteps upstairs when no one was there, and the scent of lavender was even smelled by some.

And there's a friendly ghost at the Maddermarket Theatre. The theatre was originally a Roman Catholic chapel, converted into a theatre in 1921 by Walter Nugent Monck, a founder member of the Norwich players. Nugent Monck said that every theatre worthy of the name should have a ghost. There was apparently a seat in the auditoriums that would open and shut by itself, but Nugent Monck was the first to see the theatre's ghost. Some of the confessional boxes were still standing by the stage and during a rehearsal Nugent Monck saw a monk come out of one box, cross the stage and go into a box on the other side. When he didn't reappear by the end of the rehearsal, Nugent Monck went to the box where he'd seen the monk enter, opened the door – and found nothing there.

The ghostly monk is apparently a devoted priest who wants to complete mass for his parishioners, all of whom are long since dead. The monk has since been seen by actors and crew members – and even children in the audience, one of whom apparently wrote an essay about the performance of *Agnes of God* and said his favourite bit was when the monk walked across the stage. But, of course, there is no monk in the play.

12

CRIME AND PUNISHMENT

Although most people think of prisoners of past centuries undergoing torture in chains or on the rack in a dark and damp jail, punishments were more likely to be inflicted in public, with the aim of humiliating the miscreant into good behaviour in the future. Women would be sentenced to the ducking chair for rowdiness in the street, drunkenness or using bad language. Men would be sentenced to around six hours in the stocks by the market place for disorderly behaviour and drunkenness, or even for saying the wrong thing: the mayor's Court Book for 1550–1 records that the worsted weaver John Cobbe was committed to the Cage 'with a paper upon his head for speaking of seditious words'. And his words? 'The poor can buy no corn here for the rich churls take it from them.'

But punishment wasn't as common as you would think. Although Norwich was one of the biggest cities in the country during the sixteenth and seventeenth centuries, only around seven women a year were sentenced to be ducked in the ducking stool at Fye Bridge. The mayor's Court Book for 1628–9 shows that Margaret Crookebill was ordered to be put into the cage 'for calling of Merable Church widow whore and witch and other railings' – and next time she would be ducked! Priscilla Moore was put in the cage 'for scolding and brawling with her neighbours'; and Alice Brown, alehouse keeper, was sentenced to a whipping for owing money to her brewer.

The mayor's court dealt with petty crimes or 'ill rule' such as assault, beating wives, hitting watchmen and the like. Scolds were put in the cage or ducked. People who swore had a fine of a shilling per oath or three hours in the stocks. Petty larceny (called 'michery' in the court records) and fraud meant being whipped at the post in the market place or being put in the cage. Drunkards were fined five shillings or given six hours in the stocks, or put in the house of correction (the Bridewell) if they were habitual drunkards. Lewd behaviour meant a ducking, whipping or being sent to the Bridewell – and sometimes being 'carted' round the city with a placard round your neck.

The mayor's Court Book for 1630–31 records some interesting cases.

Agnes Stonham and Ann Lacey were sentenced to the cage 'until the rising of the court' in June 1630 for 'abusing themselves by evil speeches'. Two months later, John Danyell and his wife were brought up for 'abusing Mr Sowter, a minister' – he was sentenced to the stocks and she was put in the cage. Ann Bensly and the wife of Nicholas Skyppen were committed to the cage for scolding in February 1631, and Ann Blofild shared their fate in May 1632 for 'scolding and living disorderly'. Frances Snape, wife of John, was sent to the Bridewell in May 1631 for abusing the aldermen Rosse and Hornsey, and 'for other lewdness and misdemeanours', to await her sentence. She got off reasonably lightly by being put in the stocks for drinking. Though in the same month, Anne Pory, wife of Henry, wasn't so lucky – she was sentenced to a ducking for scolding and brawling. Two months later, Mary Springold met the same fate for 'lewd and dissolute behaviour' – even though she confessed she'd wronged Nicholas Freeman and his wife and asked their forgiveness, the order stood. And Elizabeth Bromely was punished in the assembly chamber in July 1631 for speaking lewdly and wickedly against the mayor and the late Mayor Cocke.

Men were also brought to book for abusive behaviour. Thomas Kene was sentenced to six hours in the stocks for drunkenness and abusing the constable of East Wymer in July 1631, and on the same day John Bromely was whipped at the post for resisting the watch and abusing himself toward Mr Alderman Rosse, then sent back to the Bridewell.

One of the rudest cases in the book was that of Humfry Smyth in September 1630 – he swore four oaths on the Sunday in St Peter Parmentergate, and couldn't pay the fine so he was set in the stocks. But he didn't stop at that. He also beat his wife and struck the parish constable (Henry Adcock), and in the presence of eleven people 'turned down his hose and did his business', then offered to hit the ward's alderman, Mr Hornsey! He was committed to the Bridewell and 'set on work', though his wife must have had a forgiving nature as he was discharged from the Bridewell on 9 October 1630 at her request.

Other swearers simply paid up. Sayer of Pulham paid 13d towards his three-shilling fine for swearing three oaths in court in February 1631, and Thomas Maggs and John Armes paid 12d to the poor of parish for swearing in St Peter Mancroft in July 1631.

Most of the drunkards seemed to pay up or sit in the stocks. Henry Wenne of St Lawrence and John Wenne of St Michael's Coslany were convicted for drinking at Mawfrys the Cook's in July 1630; they couldn't pay so they were set in the stocks. John Atkinson met the same fate in October 1630 for drinking eight pots of beer over four hours at William Gargrave's house – and because he was an habitual drunkard, he was put in the Bridewell afterwards. Roger Nowell couldn't pay his fine in December 1630 for drinking two or three jugs of beer at the White Lyon, so he was sent to the stocks. Walter Dennys, his drinking compatriot, had a four-hour sentence in the stocks and was fined for drinking in three separate parishes.

In April 1631 Thomas Goodson was set in the stocks for drinking at house of Wiggenton and refusing to pay 3s 4d. Edward Stephenson met the same fate in June 1631 for being unable to pay the same amount of money for 'drinking contrary to law'. Thomas Mason, a former bellman, couldn't pay his five-shilling fine and had also abused Cotton's wife, so he ended up in the stocks. Robert Biggot paid twenty shillings for 'tippling without licence' in August 1630 and John Payne paid 3s 4d for drinking at Black Swan in July 1631.

The parents of illegitimate children were both condemned. Every 'lewd woman' who had a child who was chargeable to the parish was put in the Bridewell by the Justice of the Peace, punished and put to work in the Bridewell for a year. That was Elizabeth Payne's fate in June 1631, shared by Martha Rust in February 1632.

In July 1630, Thomas Ebbotts, the 'putative father of the bastard of Alice Rolfe' was committed to the Bridewell (while Alice was sent back to her master); the same sentence was handed to Jeffery Bell, 'putative father of bastard of Elizabeth Mickleburgh' a month later, and to Roger Totnell in November 1630 (although he was only 'on suspicion of bastardy' – his lover wasn't named).

Worse still was if you ran away and left your children 'on the parish' – this was known as being an 'incorrigible rogue'. In October 1630, John Welhowse was committed to the Bridewell for running away and leaving his child to the charge of the parish of St Martin at Oak.

Adultery was also condemned. In August 1630, Margaret Grove, wife of Matthew, was accused of being 'too familiarly acquainted with Robert French' – she was told not to see him again or she would be whipped. Similarly, Samuel Mason was told in May 1632 to stay away from the house of Henry Perfitt or he would be taken to the Bridewell or carted about the market place, as he was suspected of lewdness with Perfitt's wife.

But you could also be accused of lewdness with your own spouse. In November 1631, Francis Brett was told to stay away from his wife (the unusually named Munday), because he was suspected of 'having lived lewdly' with her – if he saw her again, he would be punished at the post by his own consent.

Michery often seemed to go with 'ill rule', judging by the mayor's Court Book – and the miscreants generally ended up being whipped at the post, sometimes being banished from the city or being sent to the Bridewell afterwards.

In June 1630, Robert Roberts and Faith Newton were punished in the assembly chamber and discharged from the Bridewell. Four months later, Ann Bradford and John Watson were whipped at the post; John Watson came up again for the same offence in November 1631. In June 1631 James Taylor suffered the same fate for ill rule 'and abominable disorder'. Thomas Homan was another punished at the post in October 1631, followed by the widow Alice Belton a month later and Elizabeth 'wife of Streeke' in December 1631, and John Cooke 'apprentice in Drayton' in May 1632. Agnes Goose was punished at the post and then set to work in the Bridewell in April 1632.

In November 1630, Peter Durrant had been sent to the Bridewell for idleness – a week later, he was punished there for ill rule and then banished to Ringland, just outside the city, where he came from. Thomas Collins who had lately been committed to prison for michery and ill rule was ordered to be punished in January 1632. Margaret Browne got off lightly for ill rule in November 1630 – she was simply carted. But because she swore in court at her sentencing, she was also set in the stocks!

Jane Sellars sounds a hardened case – punished at the post for ill rule in January 1631 and again at the Bridewell a week later. Though perhaps her circumstances made her that way – she was sent to the Bridewell for begging in July 1631 and was discharged in December on her promise to go to Yarmouth to get work.

Barbara Bloy was another hardened case – punished at the post for michery in November 1631, again in May 1632 and yet again a month later. And a spell in the Bridewell was the punishment for Thomas Dennys's ill rule in January 1631.

Elizabeth Reade (wife of William) was punished for michery in the assembly chamber in February 1631, as was John Cooke in July 1631, Danyell Dawbney in November 1631, Elias Hobson in January 1632, Elizabeth Giles in May 1632 and Elizabeth Ralleson at the same session.

'Disorder' was frowned on, too. Edmund Howsegoe was brought before the court in December 1630 for 'misusing his wife' but wasn't punished as he promised to 'order himself'. Clearly it wasn't one-sided because his wife also promised 'to live quietly and peaceably with him'. John Lane was committed to the Bridewell in August 1631 for 'misusing his wife', and the court added that if he beat her again, he would be 'whipped at the post by his own consent'. In April 1632, 'Widows Moore and Cragge and three others found disorderly wandering up and down city' were sentenced to six stripes in the

Bridewell, and two months later Dionis Medcalfe, wife of Silvester Medcalfe alias Parker, was kept in the Bridewell 'for disordered life'.

Disobeying your parents could have rough consequences, too – in April 1631 Elizabeth Cotton was punished in the assembly chamber for disobedience to her parents, then delivered back to her father's dwelling in the parish of St Augustine's.

Vagrancy usually meant being thrown out of the city 'with a pass' back to the vagrant's original town of birth, as the city simply couldn't cope with the influx of beggars. The charge of begging usually ended up with a whipping. Thus we have Elizabeth Downes in October 1630 and the 'wife of William Baker' a week later both being whipped in the Bridewell.

Joan Baker was sent to the Bridewell in March 1631 – and in May 1631 there's a more interesting case. Joseph Woodhowse was committed to the Bridewell for making his child go begging, until his wife came to collect him, when the Keeper of the Bridewell was instructed to release him and take her instead!

Alys Furnys added 'misbehaviour' to her charge of begging and was punished in the chamber in January 1631. Agnes Furnys – possibly a relation? – was punished at the post for begging in November 1631, as she was also convicted of 'wandering up and down'. Branch Fryer and Cragg's wife were both punished at the post for begging in July 1631, as was Ellen Dobleday in April 1632.

'Idleness' was presumably the step before begging – most people on a charge of 'living idly' were sent to the Bridwell to work, until they managed to get a job. This was the sentence for Theophilus Strange in August 1630; John Mayd two months later; Peter Durrant in November 1630; Thomas Howsego, Bryan Hudson and George Homan in December 1630; William Stockdale in February 1631 and Richard Tilles in June 1632.

On a slightly different tack, William Lister and Henry Bussey were committed to the Bridewell 'for idly wandering' in October 1630. On Christmas Day of that year Thomas Ferman was punished in the Bridewell 'for roguing abroad idly'. And John Mortymer, who was originally brought up in the glover's trade, was committed to the Bridewell in October 1631 and set to work as a glover, for 'living idly and wandering abroad with herrings'.

Runaway apprentices were treated harshly and sent back to their masters – so in October 1630 John Poynter, apprentice to John Johnson, was punished for running away (and again in the Bridewell two months later). Dennys Powle, apprentice with John Beavis, was whipped at the post in November 1631 for michery and running away. And in June 1632 John Later, apprentice to Philip Hickling, was punished and sent back to his master; because he often ran away, he was ordered to wear a pair of pothooks about his neck. The apprentice Roger Dickinson didn't run away from his master, William Ludkyn – but he was punished in the Bridewell for abusing his master in February 1631.

Stealing usually meant a fine, from Elizabethan times – and if you couldn't pay, you would be whipped. So Thomas Gabyn and John Gabyn were whipped in February 1631 for going into Cooke's garden and 'pulling up diverse roots', because they couldn't pay for the damage. Thomas Kempe cut down osiers in Carrow, again with no means of recompense, so he was 'whipped according to statute' in May 1631.

Abraham Porter and Robert Jude were set in the stocks for three hours for 'digging and carrying sand' in June 1631, but clearly it didn't stop them because Robert Porter was brought before the court for the same offence in October 1631. He was punished at the post and put in the Bridewell. His accomplice Elias Fawcett was punished at the post, and fourteen others were told to fill in the holes they'd made by 'digging of sand and undermining highways' outside St Stephen's gate, or they would be punished at the post too. A month later, John Annyson was set in the stocks for 'misbehaviour' – he'd taken some yarn at John Mandew's house, but was caught before he could carry it away.

A more interesting case was that of Thomas Clements, apprentice to Roger Brook the tailor, in September 1630. He was punished in the assembly chamber for stealing his master's money and 'other abuses'. Thomas claimed that Debra Birdsall told him to run away from his master, and had some of the money from him. Debra was brought up before the magistrates and punished in the Bridewell for taking the money. And Thomas's mother Elizabeth was also punished in the Bridewell, for 'ill counselling her son' – so parents could be held accountable for their children's actions when they were under an apprenticeship.

Cases were tried in the same place in Norwich – the Guildhall – until the 1980s, when the new courts were built at Bishopsgate and revealed a Norman stone building, the remains of which can be seen once a year on open days. And in the twentieth century, Norwich has come to the forefront in new ways of dealing with crime; two trials of electronic monitoring as a condition of bail began in Norwich Magistrates' Court and Crown Court in 1998 and 1999.

Norwich has hit the headlines in the twenty-first century, too, after Lord Woolf's ruling in December 2002 about not sending non-violent domestic burglars to prison for a first offence if their sentence would have been less than eighteen months. One of the first cases decided under this new ruling was that of Gary Callaby, a 29-year-old painter and decorator from West Raynham, near Fakenham, who used information from his customers to plan burglaries. He admitted three burglaries and asked for four others to be taken into account. At Norwich Crown Court, although Judge Alisdair Darroch wanted to give him a prison sentence, he said, 'I had to take into account the recent decision and you are fortunate in your timing.' Callaby was given a twelve-month drug treatment order, with the threat of eighteen months in prison if he breaches the terms of his drug order.

13

NORWICH'S MOST BRUTAL KILLER

James Blomfield Rush was the most notorious murderer in Norwich in the nineteenth century, although he always protested his innocence. He was known as the 'double murderer' because of his murder of Isaac Jermy, a barrister and the Recorder of Norwich, and Isaac's son Jermy Jermy.

Rush had a fairly inauspicious start to life. His mother Mary Bloomfield, the daughter of a miller and baker in Tacolneston, was engaged to a gentleman farmer near Wymondham. When the farmer backed out of the engagement, Mary was already pregnant, so she brought an action of breach of promise against him and the court awarded her heavy damages. Her son, James Bloomfield, was baptised at Tacolneston on 10 January 1800.

In September 1802, Mary married John Rush, a farmer at Old Buckenham who acted as a manager for her father, using the damages from the engagement as her dowry. Rush adopted James, so the boy became known as James Bloomfield Rush (James dropped the second 'o' as an adult), and also sent him to the grammar school in Eye.

Rush followed his stepfather into farming. In 1824 he became a tenant farmer at Aylsham under the Revd Samuel Pitman. Four years later, he married Susannah Soames and during the next twelve years they had nine children who survived infancy. After his marriage, Rush moved to Wood Dalling and rented Dalling Hall from W. Bulwer.

His first brush with the law occurred in November 1830, when there were 'Captain Swing' riots at Foulsham. Joyce, one of the men breaking up the machinery, was captured near Rush's stable. Rush called some of his men to rescue Joyce – had Joyce been tried, he would have been transported to Australia or even executed. Rush was indicted at the assizes in March 1831 for aiding a man apprehended for machine breaking, but there wasn't a formal trial and no verdict was given. Rush was discharged on condition that he kept the peace. The 'Captain Swing' rioters also set fire to stacks of wheat and straw in the area. One of Rush's wheat-stacks was destroyed by fire in 1832, and rumours abounded that he'd started the fire himself. However, he was never tried for it and the insurance office paid up – albeit less than he'd claimed for!

In 1835, Rush moved to Felmingham where he rented a farm from Revd George Preston. The following year, he also rented Stanfield Hall farm from Preston. He became close to Preston – enough for rumours to start that Preston was his natural father, though Rush himself never claimed this – and acted as Preston's agent. He also became an auctioneer and land agent. Life was looking good.

But then George Preston died in 1837 and was succeeded by his son Isaac, who was a county magistrate and Recorder of Norwich. Isaac Preston cancelled his father's leases to Rush at Felmingham and Stanfield Hall farms, on the grounds that they 'were not legally made' – then reissued them at higher rents, which Rush clearly resented. Isaac sold Stanfield Hall to Rush for £1,000, but then his ownership of Stanfield Hall was challenged by two distant relatives, Thomas Jermy and John Larner. Isaac managed to meet the challenge and then changed his name to Isaac Jermy – presumably to underline the fact that he had a valid claim to Stanfield Hall.

Meanwhile, Rush was finding money tight. He'd bought Potash Farm (next to Stanfield Hall) and had borrowed £5,000 from Isaac Jermy, which was due for payment on 30 November 1848. In 1840 he sold Stanfield Hall back to Jermy for £1,000. His stepfather died in October 1844 in a shooting accident and Rush borrowed his mother's £7,000 inheritance. A month later his wife died, leaving him to support nine children and forcing him to engage a governess, Emily Sandford.

Partly due to the money Rush owed Jermy and partly due to a long-held resentment about the leases, relationships between Rush and Jermy became strained. In early 1846, Rush allegedly said about Jermy, 'I'll not be long before I serve him with an ejectment for the other world'. By October 1847, Rush's rent for Stanfield Hall farm was in arrears, so Jermy took him to court for breach of contract and was awarded damages. When Rush had himself declared bankrupt in May 1848, Jermy took him to court again.

Rush was desperate for money. Three months later, his mother died, aged 68 – but a nurse claimed he'd poisoned his mother because he'd given her some cake moistened with something that looked like wine, a few days before her death and just after he'd been to London. He certainly had a motive for trying to get his hands on the money because he was bankrupt, the mortgage on Potash Farm was about to run out, and Emily was pregnant by him. He had nowhere to turn – except to John Larner, Isaac Jermy's enemy.

Larner promised Rush favourable leases for Potash and Stanfield Hall farms, if he would help get Stanfield Hall back. They signed an agreement in London in October 1848 which was witnessed by Emily and Larner's lawyer. Rush had also written three 'agreements' with Isaac Jermy, which were again witnessed by Emily, though the trial showed that Jermy's signature was forged.

By November 1848, Rush was clearly in a state. He complained to Emily about poachers and on 24 November he said he would go after them that evening as 'this is the night for those rascals'. He had some gin with his tea that night, then at 11.30 when he returned he said he felt unwell. Emily testified that his clothes were muddy and wet. On the Saturday he went to Felmingham and complained that some of his papers were wet; on the Sunday Emily saw Rush burning some papers. The Monday was Emily's birthday. Rush had promised to take her to a concert in Norwich, the following evening, but gave the tickets to his son and daughter-in-law instead.

Then came the fateful day – Tuesday 28 November. Rush and

Emily dined at their 'usual time' (which Emily testified was around 6 p.m.) and while she laid the cloth he went into the garden to discharge his gun. Rush was in low sprits. He claimed it was because he was 'harassed by poachers' but Emily thought there was more to it than that. When she pressed him, he said he would tell her some other time. He went into his bedroom for around fifteen minutes, then went out at 7.30 – she heard him leave but didn't see him go.

At 8 p.m., Jermy Jermy and his wife were playing cards. Isaac Jermy went to the front door (some sources say to relieve himself, which he did at the same time and in the same place every night, though the trial says it was because he 'heard a strange noise'). As soon as he opened the door, a masked man shot him at point-blank range. Evidence from Mr Nichols, the surgeon who examined Jermy's body, pointed out that the shot left a wound around three inches in diameter which shattered three ribs and blew away the entire heart. Jermy fell backwards, dead. The butler James Watson heard the shot and came out to see the gunman drop two pieces of paper in the hallway, but he was so frightened at the sight of the gunman that he scuttled back to his pantry.

Jermy Jermy heard the shot and ran to the door. The masked man shot him dead – again at point-blank range, though Jermy Jermy's wound was a mere half-inch in diameter.

Mrs Jermy went into the hall and screamed for help. Her maid, Eliza Chestney, came out to her. Eliza recognised the gunman as Rush, although he was wearing a wig and something over his face (which Watson the butler also mentioned at the trial). The masked man saw them in the passageway and shot Eliza in the hip, then shot Mrs Jermy in the arm. Mrs Jermy couldn't testify at the trial as she lay 'on a bed of suffering' – later, she had to have her arm amputated.

The masked man left the house – seen in the passageway by Margaret Read the cook and Maria Blanchflower the nurse. Watson went to a neighbour's farm for help while the other servants rallied round Mrs Jermy and Eliza. Meanwhile, a manservant in the stable swam across the moat, borrowed a horse and rode to Wymondham to send a telegraph summoning help. Armed police came straight to the hall and saw the notes left by the murderer: 'Three are seven of us here, three outside, and four inside the hall, all armed as you see us two.'

The note warned the servants not to leave the Hall or try to follow, or they would be shot – the men were 'only come to take the Stanfield Hall property'. It was signed by Thomas Jermy. Though Thomas Jermy – as Rush knew from his meetings with him and Larner in London, and pointed this out in his defence – was illiterate. So why would Rush bother writing something that could only too easily be proved a forgery?

Meanwhile, Rush returned to Potash Farm. Emily undid the bolt when he knocked at 9.30 p.m., then returned to the parlour before he came in. Rush went up to his room, then came down looking 'very much excited and . . . pale', with his boots and his coat off. He said to Emily, 'If any inquiry is made, you will say I was not out more than ten minutes.' He told her to go to bed, in her own room – usually, she shared his room – and half an hour later, she heard him moving about and then locking his door. She bolted her own door and went to sleep.

Back at Stanfield Hall, Eliza Chestney, Margaret Read and James Watson told the police they were sure the murderer was James Blomfield Rush. Blanchflower hadn't met him so she couldn't comment. The police surrounded Potash Farm at 2 a.m. – and waited.

At half past two, Rush went to Emily's room. She let him in and he reminded her that he'd only been out for ten minutes. He was trembling and she was scared and started shaking too. Rush, worried that she had a chill, got a coat to cover her. She asked him if any bad thing had happened. His reply was that he 'hoped God would bless [him], for [he] had done nothing wrong'.

At 5 a.m., when Rush's servant Solomon Savory lit a fire, the police knocked and demanded to see Rush. They arrested him, then searched the farm. They found pistols, a lantern, two cloaks (one of them a woman's cloak dyed black), bullets, shot and a wig with false whiskers. They didn't find the gun until May 1849, when the pig sheds were being cleaned out – and the gunmaker, John Field of London, said it had been specially adapted so it could be reloaded without having to be primed again. He also described the purchaser, and the description fitted Rush exactly.

Rush was taken to Norwich prison. Emily gave a statement on three occasions, each time in front of Rush – apparently at one point, Rush was 'violent' and kept moving his chair and she fainted with terror.

Finally, Rush was tried in March 1849 before Mr Baron Rolfe. According to both the *Norfolk Chronicle* and the *Norwich Gazette*, the court was packed to bursting and spectators at the trial were only allowed in with an admission ticket. The barristers had to go to court in their wigs and gowns so that 'the police on duty might admit them without interruption' and the press reporters were at the castle by 7 a.m. to take their places in the dock.

The prisoner was described as a 'powerful, well-made man' with 'a countenance in which indications of intellectual feeling are contrasted with strong animal passions'. He was charged with the murder of Isaac Jermy and answered that he was 'not guilty'. He also decided to conduct his own defence.

Eliza Chestney's statement on the first day of the trial caused a real sensation in court because she still couldn't walk – she was brought into the court in a special chair 'made for the purpose, in appearance like the crib used for the repose on an infant' and the artist for the *Norfolk Chronicle* was so impressed that he actually drew a picture of her in the chair for the newspaper. She, like the cook and the butler, said that she was sure Rush was the murderer, because both were short and had an odd gait.

Rush got particularly upset on the second day of the trial, when William Frederic Howe testified. Rush said that Howe was 'a bad man, a villainous character' and was angry the prosecution hadn't warned him about this, but the judge told him 'this is not the time' to intervene! Howe said he'd been on his way to Stanfield with three others (Maria Clarke, the laundry maid at Stanfield, plus John Todd and Thomas Howes). Clarke had gone into the house and came back with Mary Leech, one of the servants. Then Howe heard a gun and saw the flash, heard more reports and heard the alarm bell.

Emily Sandford was the next witness – her evidence took two days because she was ill and needed to rest while other witnesses gave evidence. She was allowed to use a chair in the witness box. Again, Rush was agitated and the judge said that, although he was allowed to hear the evidence, as he was defending himself, if he didn't behave the judge would throw him out of court! Emily claimed that Rush had been out that night for a lot longer than ten minutes – more like two hours, when she'd been reading a novel called *Whitefriars* and had 'read half of the volume' during his absence. She told the court that Rush had said she had to tell everyone his absence lasted only ten minutes.

She was under examination for nine and a half hours, and Rush's cross-examination took seven and a half hours! He reminded her that he'd told her, 'You should never want a home while I had one,' and that after their second child they'd planned to stop their affair – he would be the child's godfather and she would live with him as his housekeeper. Emily, in tears, replied, 'You said you never would forsake me' and claimed she'd only adopted the name of Emily James (which she'd used in the first of her two statements) as a blind to conceal the promise of marriage he'd made to her.

At last, Rush was given the chance to make his defence. His story was that a man called Joe and a lawyer had asked him to lend some men to help gain possession of Stanfield Hall for Larner and Thomas Jermy. On the evening of November 1848, he'd walked towards Stanfield to see if anything was happening, felt ill and decided to go back – and then heard three shots and the bell ringing. He went straight back to Potash Farm.

He said that you couldn't walk from Potash Farm to Stanfield Hall at night – it would mean crossing a seven-feet-wide river, a drain, then another ditch four feet wide and five feet deep. He also knew Thomas Jermy was illiterate so why would he drop the note?

After fourteen hours of listening to Rush (over the course of two days), Lord Rolfe summed up and the jury retired. They returned in ten minutes with their verdict: guilty.

On 16 April, Rush's children saw him for the last time. On 21 April, at 9 a.m. he had breakfast and then the sheriff came and took him to the condemned cell. St Peter Mancroft's bells tolled the death knell for an hour at 11 a.m., and then Rush was pinioned. He complained that the bonds were too tight and was then taken to the scaffold.

A crowd of around 20,000 people waited in the castle bailey to see him, including people from all over the country. A special excursion train bringing people from London to see the execution had been stopped at Attleborough and turned back – mainly because its occupants were the 'swell mob' and pickpockets from Whitechapel. It was a double entertainment for the gentry, who also packed out St Andrew's Hall later that night to hear Jenny Lind (known as 'the Swedish Nightingale') sing.

Rush walked calmly for twenty yards – then he raised his pinioned hands and shook his head, apparently protesting his innocence to the crowd. He mounted the scaffold without assistance, and asked Mr Pinson (the governor of the castle) if the bolt could be withdrawn while the chaplain was reading 'The grace of our Lord Jesus Christ, and the love of God, and the fellowship of the Holy Ghost, be with us, evermore.' The hangman put him under the beam and Rush said, 'For God's sake give me rope enough. Don't be in a hurry; take your time.' Then, moving his head about, he said, 'Put the knot a little higher up, don't hurry.'

The bolt withdrew, the platform fell and the crowd applauded. His body was left hanging for an hour, then was taken into the castle and a death mask was made by Giovanni Bianchi, 'a figure maker of St George's Middle Street, Norwich'. The phrenologist Mr Stark reported later that Rush's cranium 'might be mapped out' as showing great tendencies towards acquisition, aggressiveness and self-esteem; in comparison, 'cautiousness and benevolence' were small, as was hope, and 'ideality and conscientiousness' were 'very deficient'. According to Stark, Rush's perception of 'external objects and the remembrance of events' was fully developed, but his 'reflective organs' were 'exceedingly small' – he was a man who acted first and thought later.

Emily left for Australia – the money for her passage was raised by a campaign fund – and two years later married a German merchant. Rush's children were brought up by George Soames, a member of his late wife's family. Stanfield Hall passed to Sophia Jermy, Jermy Jermy's daughter – and although yet another Jermy descendant tried to claim the estate in 1870, Sophia and her husband defended themselves successfully. The hall was eventually sold out of the family in 1920.

Although Rush's execution wasn't the last public hanging in Norwich, there was so much hysteria surrounding it that the authorities considered ways of making sure there weren't so many spectators in future. From then on, hangings were carried out at eight o'clock on Monday mornings instead of noon on Saturdays.

And although Rush claimed right to the end that he was innocent, and the true murderer would be known 'in two years', all the letters claiming that the writer was the real murderer of Isaac Jermy turned out to be from cranks. So Rush's name has gone down in Norwich history as one of the city's most brutal murderers; and his death mask is on display in Norwich Castle.

14

THE DUMPLING POISONER

The case of John Stratford is particularly sad. He had the ambition and strength of character to educate himself and rise above his peasant farming roots to become an engineer at the very beginning of the nineteenth century, when poverty and rigid class boundaries made his achievement much more difficult than it would be today.

And he threw it all away by trying to murder the husband of his lover and cover up the affair, though Stratford claimed that he was simply trying to help a seriously ill man die with dignity, by putting arsenic in some flour intended for Thomas Briggs. But Briggs never got the flour because it was stolen by John Burgess, the husband of the workhouse nurse, who made dumplings for his family with the poisoned flour and died after eating them.

John Stratford was born in Postwick in 1797, the son of peasant farmers. He tended sheep as a child and was apprenticed to a blacksmith in Seething at the age of 11. His work was so good that it was described as better than that of his master's journeymen. One of the perks of being an apprentice was being given the bits of useless metal from the trade known as 'ringings and stumpings'. Stratford, keen to better himself, sold the metal to shoemakers and used the profits to buy a spelling book and paper which he then made into books so he could teach himself to read and write.

His master refused to let him burn a candle for reading – even though Stratford offered to buy the candle himself – so the young Stratford went into Seething churchyard on a moonlit night to practise his handwriting, using a tombstone as a table. It's hauntingly similar to Hardy's tale of Jude Fawley trying to educate himself, with equally tragic results.

Once Stratford's apprenticeship finished, he became a journeyman smith at Ludham – and dropped his studies in favour of what the *Norfolk Chronicle* called 'the rustic gaieties of the district'. He got married in Yarmouth in 1813 and moved to Norwich in 1817. He worked as a millwright and an engineer, then tried his hand at being a publican, becoming the landlord of the Swan in King Street. He clearly didn't enjoy the work (or wasn't good at it!) because his tenure didn't last long. He then resumed his work as a smith and built up a good business, enough to 'afford a decent subsistence for himself and his equally industrious and more prudent wife'. He had six children and was renowned as 'a kind and affectionate father'. The *Norfolk Chronicle* describes him as being 'decorous and respectful; kind in his behaviour to others', and the druggist at Stratford's trial said, 'I have known him seven or eight years; he always bore a very good character.' Eight other influential citizens testified to his good character at the trial.

So what went wrong?

At his trial, Stratford was accused of murdering John Burgess by arsenic poisoning. Stratford pleaded not guilty, because Burgess wasn't his target. And it's interesting that no one in the court brought up the fact that Burgess took flour that wasn't his.

Stratford later confessed that he intended to kill Thomas Briggs, who was in the workhouse with cancer of the face. He claimed it was a mercy killing and he was doing a favour to Briggs's wife, who didn't want him to suffer any more. But when Briggs's wife Jane took the stand, the jury heard a very different tale.

Jane Briggs said that her husband Thomas had cancer of the face and was seriously ill. He'd been in the workhouse since May 1828 and Jane had carried or sent flour to him every week. The Briggs and Stratford families were 'very intimate' and Jane was friendly with Stratford's wife – she said she was 'at [his] house perhaps three times in a week' and Stratford himself was 'several times at [her] house'. On cross-examination, Jane said that she and her husband had known Stratford for seven years on the best of terms, and she 'never knew of a word disagreeable between Stratford and my husband'.

Stratford was apparently an attractive man. According to the *Norfolk Chronicle* he was nearly six feet tall, athletic and well proportioned, but 'his legs were unsound' and his feet 'badly shaped even to deformity'. Jane Briggs had an affair with Stratford and told the court that she 'was in the family way' by him, the previous March. Stratford asked her to keep it secret as he didn't want to 'break the peace between him and his wife'. Jane said she hadn't yet told her husband and Stratford promised her that she 'should not want'.

Three weeks after Christmas (not long after Jane had had the baby, which went to full term despite Stratford's hopes that it wouldn't), Stratford went to the druggist Charles Cross to buy arsenic. He took Thomas Colman with him as a witness (which Cross said was common practice) and bought two ounces of arsenic 'for the purpose of poisoning rats'. Stratford wanted crude arsenic – apparently the strongest – but Cross only had 'powdered', so Stratford bought tuppence-worth and Cross's apprentice measured it for him and wrote 'poison' on the white and brown paper used to wrap the drug.

Susannah Hook, a 20-year-old servant at the workhouse who'd been there for two years, said that Stratford had delivered a brown-paper parcel to the workhouse, about three weeks before Burgess's death. He said the parcel was for Mr Briggs and that he didn't need to take it up himself – it would 'do quite as well' for Susannah to take it. An hour later, the workhouse nurse Rhoda Burgess came into the kitchen and Susannah gave her the parcel.

Rhoda's job was to attend Briggs, so she took the parcel to Briggs, who asked her if there was money in it. Rhoda's husband John Burgess – who apparently looked after Briggs when Rhoda couldn't – was sitting at the foot of the bed. He opened the parcel to check, but said it was just flour and put the parcel in the cupboard at the foot of Briggs's bed.

On Monday 2 March, John Burgess took the flour with the aim of 'making up the flour' – Jane Briggs's testimony was that her husband couldn't take much food other than 'thick milk', and flour was presumably the usual thickener. According to Rhoda Burgess, her husband was making flour into dumplings. Rhoda knew she had no flour in the house and she recognised the paper containing the flour as Briggs's parcel.

Burgess finished cooking the dumplings and cut them up. Rhoda noticed 'a dirty white froth on top of the water' and refused his offer of a piece of dumpling because she thought there was something wrong with it (though it isn't recorded that she tried to stop her husband eating *his* portion or nagged him about taking prisoners' belongings!). But when she saw Burgess eating heartily with no apparent ill effects, she gave two pieces of dumpling to her son, ate a piece herself and gave some to other people in the kitchen, then some to Mary Morse and Ann Pillar – presumably colleagues.

Shortly afterwards, Rhoda Burgess felt very unwell. Her husband felt 'so bad he went down to get some beer'. Half an hour later, their son helped him to bed. Burgess croaked out that he was a dying man and his eyesight was going fast. He retched, his stomach heaving, but couldn't actually be sick. Rhoda herself was violently sick.

Her son called the city surgeons, John Coleman and Robinson, to help them. Coleman realised straightaway that Burgess was dying – 'the pupils of his eyes were dilated, his body and extremities were cold, pulse hardly perceptible'. Burgess said piteously that he'd been poisoned and had made the dough himself. The son showed Coleman where the flour was and Coleman took the flour and remaining dough away. At the post-mortem, Burgess's stomach 'had all the appearances as if . . .[he'd] died from . . . a mineral poison'.

Mr Dalrymple, who carried out the post mortem, went into great detail in the trial about the procedure and the signs of arsenic poisoning. The membrane lining Burgess's stomach was highly inflamed with three deeper spots, which Dalrymple believed was caused by arsenic. Burgess's heart was full of blood 'in a fluid state' and his lungs and liver were 'gorged with blood'. Dalrymple took about ten ounces of fluid from Burgess's stomach for experimental purposes and gave it to Mr Stark, a Norwich chemist who had assisted with previous post-mortems of poison victims.

Stark testified about the forensic analysis of the flour and dough. He dried a piece of dough and applied it to a red-hot metal – the result was a 'garlic-like smell peculiar to arsenic'. He boiled another piece of dough in distilled water and mixed the cooled liquid with three different substances, all of which indicated the presence of arsenic – 'ammoniuret of silver' gave a bright yellow precipitate, 'ammoniuret of copper' gave a grass-green precipitate, and sulphurated hydrogen gave a bright lemon precipitate. Just in case the dumplings had contained salt which might affect the test, Stark tested the liquid with nitric acid, nitrate of silver and liquid ammonia – the resulting yellow liquid indicated the presence of arsenic. But when he tested the flour, there was no sign of any poison. A few days later, Stark tested the stomach contents Dalrymple had given him, first filtering out the 'solid parts'. He applied the same chemicals with similar results (though 'to a less intense degree'). He then made precipitates of the liquid of the dough, dried them and 'subject[ed] them to the process of sublimation' – producing metallic arsenic. A few days later, he 'brushed with a feather a few grains of flour from the inside of the brown paper bag', tested the flour and discovered traces of arsenic.

Thomas Briggs testified at the trial with a veil over his face, 'such was its dreadful appearance produced by cancer'. He said, 'I mostly lie in bed with my face covered' and he hadn't seen Burgess take the flour. Several witnesses testified that no person had access to Briggs's room. Jane Briggs told the court that her husband knew all about the pregnancy, but Stratford hadn't known this.

At this point in the trial, Stratford claimed his innocence. Nine local worthies gave him 'a most excellent character for honesty, humanity and industry'. The jury retired – then asked Mr Justice Parke to clear up one point for them. His answer was that no, there was no evidence that any flour was taken from Briggs's bag before Burgess made the dumpling.

The jury pronounced Stratford guilty of the crime of wilful murder. They said, 'either to carry on that criminal connection which appears to have existed, or to conceal its result', Stratford intended to murder Thomas Briggs. Although Stratford failed in his objective, John Burgess died as a result, so Stratford was condemned to death, 'hanged by [his] neck until [he was] dead, and that [his] body be dissected.'

At midnight, Stratford was taken back to the gaol and given 'some trifling articles of nourishment' along with the bread and water allowed to prisoners under sentence of death. Early the next morning, he was visited by Charles Millard, the prison chaplain. On the Saturday, one of the city sheriffs called and persuaded him to confess the truth – Stratford was in tears at this point and blamed what happened on his 'reading of infidel publications' (including Paine's *Age of Reason*).

Stratford's confession was witnessed by Charles F. Millard, the chaplain at Norwich Gaol. Stratford said he'd only bought an ounce of arsenic from Cross (and paid him two pence). From talking to Jane Briggs, he knew she sent flour to Thomas in the workhouse. And she'd said to Stratford, 'What a blessing it would be if God would release him from his sufferings.' Stratford also knew that Jane was pregnant by him. He had a third of an ounce of crude arsenic, which he said he'd received from the person for whom he worked – clearly not the same as the arsenic he'd bought from Cross, which presumably he'd already used to kill rats. He powdered the arsenic, sifted it through a piece of rag into some flour, put the flour into a bag, tied it up and took it to the workhouse at 11 a.m. on Wednesday 11 February. He gave it to Susanna Hook at the kitchen door and told her it was for Thomas Briggs.

Strangely, he claimed, 'It did not occur to me at this time that I was committing any crime, but when I went to bed, such terrors seized my mind that I could not sleep.' He then said, 'My object was to destroy Briggs, from the fear that the exposure of my intimacy with the woman Briggs would break the peace between my wife and me.' Throughout, he'd always spoken of his wife as 'a loving, faithful, frugal and industrious wife; a virtuous woman, and an exemplary mother'.

Stratford's family came to visit him that afternoon – his wife, six children, his two brothers and their wives, and four other relations. They stayed with him for nearly two hours, and his 4-year-old daughter was delighted to see her daddy again and wanted him to go home with her 'to tea'. Her words broke Stratford's heart and his wife comforted him.

The morning after the conviction, Mr Paraman, the governor of Norwich Gaol, went to London to find 'an experienced executioner'. He returned on the Sunday night and Stratford asked him to read the Bible to him. Later that day, Stratford told one of the gaolers that there was a pamphlet in a drawer at his house – 'One of Carlisle's blasphemous publications' (that is, Richard Carlisle, revolutionary and advocate of free speech – Shelley wrote a letter about him in 1820 which was considered so dangerous that it wasn't actually published until 1990!) – and made the gaoler promise to find it and burn it so his children would not read it and be affected.

Stratford couldn't rest that night. By five o'clock the next morning, there were nearly three hundred people by the outer gates to the prison, waiting to view the execution, and 'the crowd kept rapidly increasing'. At ten, the bell rang for the chapel service. Stratford gave his hat, cap and comb to the three prisoners who had shared his cell before the trial. After the service, he was led round the chapel to say goodbye to his fellow prisoners and was led back to his cell, where he prayed for a quarter of an hour and was visited by the mayor. His arms were pinioned and he walked to the foot of the drop, 'walking firmly and with a steady countenance the whole way'.

When the hangman put the rope round his neck, Stratford fretted that the knot was on the wrong side – presumably fearing that his death would therefore be slow and agonising. The hangman reassured him, then put the cap over Stratford's head. The executioner drew the bolt at the signal of a handkerchief during the chaplain's reading of the Lord's Prayer. Stratford's end was quick; and had been watched by a crowd 'extended back into St Giles' Street as far as it was possible to catch a glimpse of the gallows'. According to the *Norfolk Chronicle*, spectators lined the windows and roofs of the neighbouring houses and even the battlements of the church steeple at St Giles.

Stratford's body was then taken down, stripped and taken to the Guildhall in a cart for exposure to public view. Several thousand people (women as well as men!) went to see it over the course of two hours. His body was then taken to the Norfolk and Norwich hospital for dissection. Mr Mazzotti, the modeller, took a cast from the head and neck 'for craniological purposes', and a phrenologist commented that 'Stratford's brain is one of the finest and firmest that I ever saw dissected'. The surgeon Mr Cross delivered several anatomical lectures on Stratford's body, to what appears to be large audiences, including 'a great many medical pupils'.

After Stratford's death, J. J. Gurney published a tract about him. He said that Stratford was 'endued with excellent sense and good natural talents, and his mind was more cultivated than is generally the case with persons of the labouring class'. Stratford was known as 'one of the ablest working mechanics in the city', diligent, and 'for many long years a good husband, and a kind considerate parent'. According to Gurney,

> Stratford, under the fatal guidance of false principles – under the pernicious tuition of a Payne and a Carlisle – renounces public worship; breaks the Sabbath; connects himself with gamblers; becomes the companion of sinners, faithless to an exemplary wife, an adulterer, and in the end, *a Murderer*.

But it doesn't answer the real question. Why did Stratford want to kill Thomas Briggs? Was it because he'd fallen in love with Jane (bearing in mind his own avowal that he didn't want to 'break peace' with his wife – and they were clearly on good terms, judging by his last day) or was it a mercy killing because Thomas Briggs was his friend and was clearly suffering?

The answer is tantalisingly lost to history. The reporters of the *Norfolk Chronicle* say that before he wrote his confession, Stratford 'entered at some length into an explanation of the circumstances which had led to his criminal connection with the woman Briggs, but which we purposely omit to detail'. We will never, ever know.

15

THE BILL-HOOK MURDERESS

Martha Alden was one of only three women hanged at Norwich Castle in the nineteenth century. She was convicted of murdering her husband and there was less than a fortnight between her committing the crime and the sentence being carried out. She killed Samuel Alden on 18 July 1807, was tried at the summer assizes and hanged on 31 July 1807.

A broadsheet sold at her hanging for 1d noted that Martha was 32 years old, married for fourteen years and had five children, one of whom was born before her marriage and three of whom predeceased her. By sad coincidence – and not mentioned in the broadsheet – two of the children died on the same day of the year, 13 December, two years apart.

Martha Alden was born in Cambridgeshire into a family with a small farm; her four brothers and three sisters outlived her. Her husband Samuel is described in the *Newgate Calendar* as 'a husbandman . . . accounted a quiet, industrious character.' However, the broadsheet tells a very different story – that the Aldens 'had frequently very violent disputes'. Martha testified at the trial that her grandfather had left her husband £50. This money was meant for Martha, but the legacy was well before the Married Women's Property Act came into force, so the money went straight to her husband. Samuel Alden spent it on drink and this was the cause of their first set of arguments, as he wasn't 'sufficiently industrious to support his family'. So it's small wonder that their house consisted of just two rooms, a kitchen and a bedroom, with a narrow corridor in between. The rooms were cramped, too – one witness estimated the size of the bedroom as only seven feet by ten.

At the trial, according to the broadsheet, Martha said that she had 'long wished to be rid of her husband, having a regard for another man' and also 'was very vicious in receiving other men to her bed beside her husband'. But that wasn't the reason why she murdered him: it was because on the night of the murder, he said to her 'that, if it were not for the law, he would kill her'. And so Martha had a stark choice: kill or be killed, because how could she be certain that the drunken Samuel would stay on the right side of the law?

The day started normally enough for the Aldens. Samuel Alden spent Saturday 18 July 1807 drinking in the White Horse pub in Attleborough. Martha was with him and her 7-year-old child for a while, but left Samuel at the pub and he carried on drinking until nearly midnight, when he walked home with Edmund Draper. Draper, the first witness at the trial, stated that he'd been drinking with Samuel but was 'perfectly sober at that time', whereas Samuel was 'rather fresh, but sober enough to walk, staggering a little'. When they arrived at the Alden house, Draper noticed 'there was a larger fire burning on the hearth in the kitchen than was usual at that time of year'. But Alden seemed 'in good health' and 'no ill words passed between . . . [them] in his presence'. The only people Draper saw in the house were Martha, Samuel and a 7-year-old boy. So Draper went home towards Thetford.

Alden went to bed, drunk; he was lying asleep on his side on the outside of the bed when Martha struck him twice with a bill-hook. According to the broadsheet, 'he never spoke, sighed, nor moved hand or foot' – and at the time the child was asleep in a neighbouring room, presumably either the corridor or the kitchen. Martha's own confession states that on the Saturday night, her husband was 'a good deal in liquor' and they quarrelled. He threatened to beat her and then threw himself on the bed. No doubt this was a frequent occurrence, as Martha Alden was clearly a battered wife. And 'at that instant she formed the resolution of destroying him'. So she ran into the next room and came back with the bill-hook, which she held in both hands. She struck him on the forehead and throat 'with her utmost strength' and Samuel died instantly.

Then it sank in what she'd done. She'd murdered her husband. There was blood everywhere – not to mention a body. How was she going to conceal what had happened? And people were going to start asking questions when Samuel didn't turn up for work. What was she going to do?

Clearly she spent the rest of the night wandering about, because one of the first witnesses of the trial, Charles Hill, said that he met her somewhere around three o'clock in the morning on Sunday 19 July 1807. Hill had risen to go to see his daughter ten miles away at Shelfanger Hall. It was wet, so he took the turnpike road towards Thetford and passed the Alden house. He saw the door was open and Martha was standing nearby. She accosted him, saying, 'I cannot think what smart young man it was coming down the common.' Hill gave no hint as to her tone. Was she drunk, coquettish – or in a complete and utter panic?

When Hill asked her what she was doing at this time of night, she claimed she'd been down to the pit in her garden (on the opposite side of the road) for some water. She also said she'd been at the White Horse with her husband and Draper and hadn't been home for long – she claimed they'd all come home together but her husband had gone somewhere.

Through the open doorway, Hill saw some old cloths lying in a heap by the hearth and asked what they were. Martha told him they were covering her little boy, who was asleep. She then said that her husband's brother was going into Essex and Samuel had said he would go with him. Hill reminded her that her husband had 'let himself to harvest to Mr Parson' and added that if he went to Essex, he would not be back in time for the harvest. Martha said, 'I know he will never come back, and if he has got a job, he never will settle to it.'

Around 6 a.m., Martha went to a near neighbour's house, where her friend Mary Orvice and her father lived. Martha asked Mary to walk home with her. As soon as they arrived at the Alden house, Martha turned to Mary and confessed, 'I have killed my husband.' She took Mary into the ground-floor bedroom to show her Samuel's body.

Mary was shocked to see that Samuel was indeed dead, with his face severely cut and his head almost severed from the body. The wall next to the bed was covered in blood, as was the bedpost at the feet. The chimney-piece also had blood on it, and Mary said at the trial that the walls of the corridor leading from the bedroom to the outside door were 'much sprinkled on each side' with blood. The smell must have been incredible. Even more damningly, there was a blood-stained hook next to the body. Martha produced a 'common corn-sack' and asked Mary to hold it while she put the body into it.

Martha then dragged the body out of the bedroom, through the corridor and kitchen, out of the house, across the road and pushed it into the ditch surrounding the garden – according to Mary, there was already a grave there that Martha had dug, around six feet long and nineteen inches deep. It was much too shallow to hold a body – but Martha had reached a layer of clay soil and wasn't strong enough to dig through it to make the grave deep enough. Once the body was in place, Martha put some mould over the body to hide it temporarily and left it.

Shortly afterwards – some time between six and seven – Martha met William Parsons Jr., while walking with Mary on the Turnpike Road. Martha told him that she'd lost her husband and that 'two men in sailor's habits' had gone past her house at around 2 a.m. She'd told them that if they overtook a man on the road they should send him back, but 'they only gave her a dirty answer and passed on', and Martha explained that she was worried that Samuel was either murdered or drowned.

Mary then left and went to Larling. According to the broadsheet, that night Mary suggested that Martha slept at their house so she would not have to be alone.

On the morning of Monday 20 July Martha saw William Parsons again. For the second time, she told him that she'd lost her husband and had 'been above thirty miles that day to look for him'.

Later that evening, Martha called to see one of her neighbours, the widow Sarah Leeder, and asked to borrow a spade – she claimed that a neighbour's sow had broken into her garden and rooted up potatoes. Presumably Samuel had sold the Aldens' own spades – surely a 'husbandman' would have his own tools? And indeed Martha was seen digging in her garden by Mary Parker, another neighbour. When Mary Parker asked her what she was doing, Martha said that Mrs Leeder's cow (possibly a misprint in the newspaper report for 'sow') had got in and spoiled her potatoes. But Mary Parker saw Martha digging in the ditch, and there were no breaks in the fence – only patches of mould showing where Martha had climbed the fence.

Mary Orvice had stayed with Martha all day, until it was dark, and then at 10 p.m. they went into the garden. Martha opened up the grave, took out the body (which the newspaper describes as that of 'a small man') and dragged it along the ground in its sack for 390 yards to the edge of the clay pit on the common. She then 'shot the body into it out of the sack', and took the sack away with her. She said nothing else to Mary Orvice and they both went home.

On the morning of Tuesday 21 July, Mary went to the Alden house and helped Martha clean up, taking some warm water and even scraping the wall next to the bed as well as helping Martha wash the quilt. Martha took up some loose straw and told Mary that she was going to throw it into Mr Parsons's ditch because it was bloody. She warned Mary not to say a word to anyone about it, or Mary 'would certainly be hanged' as well. But that evening, Mary was clearly overcome by guilt and confessed all to her father. The judge ruled that Mary's testament was suspect, as she was an accessory to the attempted concealment of murder – but as most of her descriptions matched those of the other witnesses, it was allowed to stand.

At 11 p.m. on the Tuesday night, Sarah Leeder went to find some missing ducks. It seems an odd time to go looking for ducks – even in the middle of July and allowing for the moonlight, it would be too dark to see ducks properly at 11 p.m. in a place still unlit by gas lamps. But Sarah found her ducks in a small pit; next to it, near Wright's Plantation, there was a larger pit and Sarah saw something floating in it. She poked the object with a stick and it sank and rose again – but despite the bright moonlight the place was in shadow and she couldn't work out what it was, so she went home. On the morning of Wednesday 22 July, Sarah went back and poked the thing with a stick – to her horror, two hands came up, with the arms of a shirt stained with blood! She concluded it was a murdered man and, shrieking, she ran home and told a young lad to go and tell all the neighbours what she'd found.

Shortly after, she returned to the pond and discovered that the body had been brought out. She recognised it as Samuel Alden's – 'his face was dreadfully chopped and his head cut very nigh off'. She said that the body was wearing an old coat, 'with a slop or shirt over it', but no shoes, stockings or breeches; she claimed that the shirt was turned over the head. The body was put in a cart and taken to the Alden house. Sarah went looking for the spade she'd lent Martha and found it next to a hole in the ditch surrounding the Aldens' garden – a hole which she claimed at the trial looked like a shallow, open grave with blood around it. Sarah also went into the bedroom in the Alden house and saw blood on the bed's feet, the ticking and the wall against which the bed stood.

The Attleborough parish constable gave orders to Edward Rush to search the Alden house that same day. Rush found a bill-hook 'in a dark chamber' and it seemed to have blood on the handle and the blade, though the blade looked as if it had been washed. William Parsons also searched the house and added that the chimney board, on the opposite side of the room to the bed, was marked with 'blood stains which bore the appearance of an attempt having been made to scrape them off with a knife'. He said that the passage between the bedroom and kitchen had blood in places, and there were bloodstains on one of the bed's feet – he took the wood and produced it in court as evidence. He also saw a sack on the bed with spots of blood on it, and a piece of another sack which had been washed. In the shed next to the house, he found another sack 'concealed underneath nearly a hundred flags of turf'.

The parish officers asked Mr Marner, the surgeon, to examine Samuel Alden's body. Marner described the wounds as 'a deep and mortal wound round the neck, reaching from ear to ear, and an extensive and deep cut across the forehead, and another cut down the left cheek, by which the jaw was broken.' Marner added that the wounds couldn't possibly be self-inflicted.

The report in the *Norfolk Chronicle* does not mention either Martha's supposed 'regard for another man' or her bed-hopping habits, but the judge at the trial said that 'he had never before met with a case so horrid and atrocious'. The reports 'add, with sorrow and concern, that the behaviour of the wretched woman . . . appears . . . to be influenced by that hardened and remorseless spirit . . . sunk to the lowest stage of degradation and depravity.'

The trial lasted for three hours. The court was crowded and hot ('several of the female part of the audience were overpowered by . . . [the heat] and obliged to be carried out'), and the jury reached their verdict in a very short time – guilty.

The judge pronounced the sentence: Martha was to be 'drawn on a hurdle to the place of execution, there to be hanged by the neck till she was dead, and her body afterwards to be dissected'. Martha made it clear that Mary Orvice had nothing to do with the murder, and had just helped her to put the body in the sack when asked.

The *Newgate Calendar* concludes,

On Friday, 31 of July, at twelve o'clock, this unhappy female was drawn on a hurdle, and executed on the castle hill, pursuant to her sentence, in presence of an immense concourse of spectators. She behaved at the fatal tree with the decency becoming her awful situation.

16

KETT'S REBELLION

In the summer of 1549, Norwich became the focus for the country's politics when the government was sent into a panic by an uprising led by Robert Kett. There was interest abroad, too – Emperor Charles V was concerned about the unrest and his ambassador was afraid that the four hundred cavalry he'd lent the English to deal with the Scots would be used against the Norfolk rebels instead. And with good cause, because foreign mercenaries did make quite a large contribution to the eventual defeat of Kett – including some from Germany, Italy, Switzerland and the Netherlands.

So why did Kett's rebellion start? As with many of the uprisings in southern England, it was all to do with the practice of enclosure, where local landowners started fencing off part of the common lands for their own profit.

The common pasture was actually the property of the lord of the manor, though he was supposed to leave enough land unenclosed to meet the needs of his freehold tenants – common grazing often meant the difference between starvation and survival. But as many tenants didn't have freehold, their needs were ignored.

The demand for wool increased, so more landowners enclosed tracts of land, turned them over to sheep production and kept large flocks. Unemployment rocketed as only one shepherd was needed instead of ten labourers. Taxation increased to pay for war against Scotland and France; prices and rents soared. Droughts, a dramatic rise in the population and the move from arable farming to sheep farming led to food shortages. Protector Somerset had set up the Enclosure Commission in 1547 to investigate what was happening and to stop the abuses, but the commission was seen as toothless, because of powerful opposition by the gentry.

There were riots in Norfolk over enclosures in Fakenham in 1520 and 1525, Walsingham in 1537 (suppressed virtually as it started) and Hingham in 1539; then Griston in 1540, Great Dunham in 1544 (with talk of risings in Buckenham, Fincham and Swaffham); and finally in Great Yarmouth, Middleton and King's Lynn in 1548. They all failed because they didn't have a leader.

But then in 1549 the common people found a man who would lead them.

Robert Kett.

1549 was a tumultuous summer throughout the country. Everywhere the poorer people pulled fences down. Somerset promised a general pardon to fence-breakers but they ignored him and continued pulling down fences. In July he told local officials to suppress the riots.

And then the biggest single rising started.

Part of the trouble was an old family rivalry between the Flowerdews and the Ketts. The lawyer John Flowerdew (who lived at Stanfield Hall, the location of another tragedy three hundred years later) looted Wymondham Abbey in 1536 when Henry VIII closed it. He stole the lead from the roof, damaging the parish church, and ignored the agreement between the King and the town about Wymondham's rights in the Abbey. Kett, who was closely involved with the parish church, opposed Flowerdew's actions. Even when the Abbey question was settled, there was still resentment between them. Flowerdew was also in debt to William Kett, Robert Kett's elder brother.

When the rebels started taking down fences and ditches around Wymondham, Flowerdew feared for his own enclosures and bribed the rebels with forty pence to take down Kett's fences instead. But Kett shocked the rebels by joining them. He realised how unjust enclosure was, and said, 'Whatever lands I have enclosed shall be made common unto ye and all men, and my own hand shall first perform it.' And then he helped the rebels demolish Flowerdew's fences. He'd stood up against Flowerdew despoiling the abbey; now he was standing up for another cause in which he believed, even though it threatened his own livelihood. He even said he was ready 'to sacrifice my substance' and 'my very life itself' in the cause.

On 9 July his followers met under an oak tree that still exists by the old A11. They marched to Norwich and made a camp at Bowthorpe. The Sheriff of Norfolk and the Mayor of Norwich tried to disperse them but failed.

On 10 July, the rebels went to Eaton and asked for permission to pass through the city to make camp at Mousehold Heath. The city councillors refused and the rebels drew up their complaint: 'What we want is liberty, and the power, in common with our so-called superiors, of enjoying the gifts of nature.'

The next day, they crossed the river at Hellesdon and captured Sir Roger Wodehouse, who had tried to bribe them with food and drink to go home. They camped in Drayton, then marched to Mousehold Heath and occupied Surrey House (which had been under Flowerdew's control, as the royal Escheator) and the deserted St Michael's Chapel, which became known as 'Kett's Castle' and gave an excellent view over Norwich.

The camp stayed at Mousehold for seven weeks, swelling to around 15,000 strong by the end. Kett set up an alternative government, with two 'governors' elected to represent each of the twenty-four Hundreds in the county. He encouraged his men to build turf huts and wooden shacks, and set out warrants in the King's name, written in legal terms, authorising his followers to commandeer food. But no looting or abuses were allowed – he stated that 'no violence or injury be done to any honest or pooreman'.

The food was shared out publicly under the Oak of Reformation, which was also a court of justice where complaints were heard. Religious services were preached every day from the same point – Kett's men were ordered and disciplined, not a rabble. When they held trials of gentry accused of making enclosures, there were no hangings, and the prisoners were simply kept in Surrey House.

Kett and his followers drew up a list of twenty-nine requests.

Enclosure wasn't their only grievance. The rebels asked the king to stop the practice of enclosure and rack renting, make the measurements of bushels the same throughout the country (eight gallons), remove priests who didn't preach properly and make those earning more than £10 a year teach the children of the poor. Their most famous request was that 'all bond men may be made free, for God made all free with his precious blood shedding'. The rebels didn't want to overthrow society – they wanted to make it socially and economically just. This is a far cry from Holinshed's view of the rebels as 'wicked caitiffs' and ignorant.

The royal herald arrived on 21 July and offered a pardon, provided the rebels dispersed – and the King's reply to the twenty-nine requests offered nothing. Kett refused the pardon, saying, 'Kings and princes are wont to pardon wicked persons, not innocent and just men. We . . . are guilty ourselves of no crime.' The herald realised he couldn't arrest Kett because the rebel forces were too big. So he retired to Bishopgate Bridge, closed it and packed it with earth, and put guards on the rest of the city gates. Kett didn't want bloodshed and offered a truce, but it was rejected. The rebels attacked the bridge and swam the river. Norwich fell to the rebels, who opened the bridge again and took military stores back to the camp.

The herald offered a second pardon, which Kett refused as 'empty promises'. The herald left for London, leaving Kett in charge of the city and his rebels guarding strategic points. Any looting was quickly stopped and there was little destruction; any captured men were simply held prisoner, not killed or harmed.

Somerset meanwhile ordered the Earl of Northampton to raise an army and march to Norwich. On 31 July, with Northampton's army outside the city gates, the royal herald ordered Kett to surrender. Kett knew he had the backing of some of the people in the city as well as his own rebels, so he refused. A three-hour battle ensued. According to a near-contemporary account by Alexander Neville, 'Many [rebels] were drowned in their own and other men's blood.' Three hundred rebels died and the rebels withdrew to Mousehold.

The next morning, Northampton offered another pardon at the

Pockthorpe gate of the city. It was rejected by Flotman, one of the rebel leaders, on the same basis as Kett's earlier reply, that they weren't traitors and wanted justice from the gentry. While this was happening, more rebels stormed Bishopgate Bridge again and captured the royal cannons. Lord Sheffield, Northampton's deputy, was unhorsed and killed by Fulke the butcher and his comrades, and by noon the royal forces withdrew. Kett's rebels overran the city and fires were set at several city gates, Bishopsgate and the hospital. According to Sotherton's account, the rebels looted shops and warehouses, and made the citizens bake them bread and pasties to stop them looting the rest of their goods.

Kett eventually persuaded them to stop. He realised that Somerset was bound to send another royal force and tried to increase his power base by capturing Great Yarmouth, but his attempts failed.

On 18 August, a second royal army marched to Norwich – this time, 7,500 strong and led by the Earl of Warwick. The gentry of Essex, Suffolk and Norfolk joined him and the army was 12,000 strong when it reached Norwich on 24 August.

Warwick's herald, Gilbert Dethick, offered a pardon to all the rebels except Kett, but their initial greetings of 'God Save the King' changed when the herald said their 'vile and horrible company' must accept the pardon or be crushed because Warwick would never 'depart out of the place till without pity and mercy he had vanquished them with the sword'. Some of the rebels tried to intimidate the herald; Kett led Dethick to one side so he could read the pardon again, but Kett's attempts to quieten the situation backfired in the most unexpected way.

A boy turned his back to the herald and bared his buttocks. The herald's bodyguard was so angry that he shot the boy, and the rebels burst out in uproar. They let the herald go back to Warwick, then closed the city gates. Kett tried to go with the herald to negotiate a settlement, but some of the rebels came after them, demanding to know where Kett was going and saying that 'we will go with you, and with you will live and die'.

Warwick's soldiers forced their way through St Stephen's Gate and the Brazen Doors, killing many rebels. Forty-nine rebels were hanged in the market place later that day.

The rebels managed to capture the royal cannons when the artillery got lost in the maze of streets, but another three hundred rebels were killed by royal forces near St Andrew's Hall. By sunset, the rebels were driven back to their camp and Warwick held Norwich.

The next day, the rebels tried to recapture Norwich but Warwick kept them out. On 26 August, the Lansknechts (lance knights) arrived – 1,400 well-trained German mercenaries, the best troops in Europe, who had been going to fight against the Scots. The rebels decided to leave their camp and fight on open ground, trusting in an ancient prophecy that they would win if they fought at Dussindale:

> The countrie gnuffes, Hob, Dick, and Hick,
> With clubs and clowted shoone,
> Shall fill vp Dussin dale with bloud
> Of slaughtered bodies soone.

They prepared for battle in darkness, hoping to gain an advantage over Warwick. The next morning, Warwick again offered a pardon to everyone except the leaders. It was rejected. The first shot by the rebels brought down the royal standard-bearer, hitting him in the leg and killing his horse. And then Warwick unleashed his mercenaries, who completely routed the rebels – over three thousand died, whereas Warwick only lost around two hundred and fifty soldiers and seven gentlemen. By 4 p.m. on 27 August, the battle was over.

Warwick sent a pardon to Kett's forces. They were suspicious and said they would only believe it if they heard the pardon from Warwick himself, so Warwick rode out to them to give them the pardon personally.

Meanwhile, Kett fled. He was found in a barn at Swannington, a few miles outside the city, on 28 August and brought back to Norwich. The man who found him was awarded twenty shillings by the Privy Council on 3 February 1550. The rebel leaders were hanged, drawn and quartered and their heads were fixed to towers around the city. Around three hundred rebels were executed but then Warwick asked the gentry, 'Would you be ploughmen yourselves and harrow your own land?' Realising that they were killing off their labourers, the gentry stopped the executions.

The cleaning-up took three weeks – 248 cart-loads of rubbish were taken from the market place alone, and it took three men seventeen days to bring twenty-four loads of thorns from Hethel and then re-ditch and hedge Town Close, whose fences were pulled down when Kett's rebels first came to Norwich.

Robert Kett and his brother William were taken to the Tower of London. They were tried on 26 November and both were found guilty of treason. They were sentenced to be hanged at Tyburn, cut down while still alive, disembowelled, their entrails burned, their heads cut off and their bodies quartered. Then it was decided they should be executed in Norfolk, so the Sheriff of Norfolk, Sir Edmund Windham, brought them back to Norwich and they were put in chains in the Guildhall dungeons.

On 7 December, Robert Kett was taken in chains to Norwich Castle. He was hauled up alive from the ground, hanged from the walls and his body left there as a warning – it stayed there until the next summer, when townspeople complained of the smell in the hot weather, and then he was buried in an unmarked grave. William Kett was hanged from the steeple at Wymondham Abbey. Their properties were forfeited to the crown.

Somerset was executed for treason in 1552. Warwick became the most powerful man in England, but when he tried to prevent the accession of Mary Tudor, he found himself isolated. Norwich was one of the first cities to proclaim Mary as queen, mainly because of the way Warwick treated the rebels in 1549. Warwick ended his life on the scaffold in 1553.

The city records – proceedings of the municipal assembly – say that on 27 August 1549, the Earl of Warwick 'upon Mousehold Heath vanquished Robert Kett . . . from their most wicked rebellion, and did suppress them, and delivered this city from the great danger, trouble and peril.' In thanksgiving, they decreed that on 27 August every year the shops in the city should be shut and all citizens should go to their parish church when the bells rang at 7 a.m., and pray to God and for the king in remembrance of their deliverance. Each parish was to ring a 'solemn peal with all their bells' and then everyone was allowed to depart 'to his occupation or other business'. The practice was continued for well over a hundred years – and there was even a festival of deliverance as late as August 1728.

However, over the years people came to recognise that Kett wasn't a traitor – he was simply fighting for justice. And in 1949, the citizens of Norwich placed a tablet on the Castle 'in reparation and honour to a notable and courageous leader in the long struggle of the common people of England to escape from a servile life into the freedom of just conditions.'

17

THE GREAT BLOW

During the Civil War, Norwich didn't suffer sieges such as those at York, Bristol and Exeter. There wasn't a garrison here, or any raiding or plundering. But even though Norwich was right in the middle of Parliamentarian territory, the citizens weren't united behind Parliament. There were sixteen executions for rebellion, several riots, recruiting, heavy taxation and ransacking of churches – including the cathedral. The biggest event of the war for Norwich was probably the 'Great Blow' of 1648, which caused around a massive £20,000 of damage, equivalent to £1.6 million in today's money.

Norwich started off very much on the side of Parliament. In July 1642, when Captain Moses Treswell rode to Norwich and read the Commission of Array to recruit royalist volunteers, the mayor's court forbade him to beat his drum – then actually imprisoned him, and delivered him to Parliament on a bond of £100. Their actions were approved by Parliament in August 1642. In the same month, the mayor's court ordered a double watch set every day at 9 p.m., with the city gates locked. They also sent 470 lbs of gunpowder to London 'to be exchanged for the best sort' and put it, plus arms, above the assembly chamber.

In March 1643, the mayor of Norwich, William Gostlin, was arrested for royalist sympathies – he'd refused to seize 'all malignants' horses in the whole city'. He was taken to Cambridge by Lord Grey of Warke, and the remainder of the aldermen were ordered to seize horses (though they allowed several royalist sympathisers to 'buy back' their horses, such as John Lowe who paid £10 for his two horses, and Alexander Anguish who paid £8 for one horse). Later that month, Augustine Holl's attempt at a royalist insurrection was suppressed very quickly by Lieutenant Craske, who threatened to blow his house up if he didn't surrender himself and his men. Prices rose swiftly and coal was so expensive that the brewers had to use 'furze brakes' in the manufacture of beer. Parliament meanwhile demanded more and more taxes. Norwich was supposed to raise £53 a week – on 11 September 1643, the mayor's court ordered aldermen to collect 'voluntary' contributions for Lord Fairfax in the north and take the name of anyone who refused. Two months later, Norwich was rebuked for not confiscating royalist estates quickly enough, and the state papers actually refer to the 'lukewarmness' of Sir John Potts in sequestering estates.

In September 1643, Parliament decided to rid churches of anything connected with Roman Catholicism. The city records for January 1644 show that the aldermen were told to go to all the churches in the city and 'take notice of all such scandalous pictures crucifixes and images' and 'demolish' them, and 'take the names of all such persons as can give any information of any misdemeanour of Scandalous Ministers'. Various items were burned publicly in the market place in March 1644 – the mayor's court book refers to 'seven popish pictures' taken from St Swithin's, the 'angel and four evangelists' from St Peter's, 'Moses and Aaron and four evangelists' from the cathedral and 'some other superstitious pictures'. Four months later, the municipal assembly ordered Stump Cross at St Saviour's to be burned and the stones taken 'for the use of the city'.

In March 1644, the mayor's court sent a letter to the Dean of the cathedral, ordering him to 'pull down all pictures and crucifixes yet undemolished' and 'repaye and make up the windows' which had been already taken out or were against the ordinance of parliament. Bishop Hall wrote of it in *Hard Times*:

> The Sheriff Toftes and Alderman Linsey, attended with many zealous followers, came into my chapel to look for superstitious pictures and relics of idolatry . . . it is no other than tragical to

relate the carriage of that furious sacrilege . . . Lord, what work was here, what clattering of glasses, what beating down of walls, what pulling down of seats, what wresting out of irons and brass from the windows and graves, what defacing of arm, what demolishing of curious stone work . . . what tooting and piping upon the destroyed organ pipes, and what a hideous triumph in the market day before all the country, when in a kind of sacrilegious and profane procession, all the organ pipes, vestments, both copes and surplices, together with the leaden cross, which had been newly sawn down from the green yard pulpit, and the service books and singing books that could be had were carried to the fire in the public market place.

Today, you can still see graffiti in the cathedral scratched into the bays by the musketeers; heads of some statues are missing and there is a musket ball lodged in Bishop Goldwell's tomb. Though the Despenser reredos in St Luke's chapel managed to survive the Puritans, as it was used upside down as a table in the workshop of the cathedral carpenter.

The Puritans didn't think it was enough and called for the cathedral to be pulled down – and some even suggested that the stones should build a new pier at Great Yarmouth. But when Charles II was restored in 1660 the cathedral was returned to the Dean and Chapter.

Post-war accounts say Captain Garrett exercised his soldiers on horseback in the cathedral on Christmas Day. Joseph Hall refers to 'the cathedral now open on all sides to be filled with musketeers, waiting for the major's return, drinking and tobacconing as freely as if it had turned alehouse'. Another captain, Major Sherwood, exercised his foot company in the choir area and they turned their backs upon the altar, 'lifting up their bumbs [sic] and howlding down their heads against it in a deriding manner'. The accounts are Royalist and heavily biased, and they claim that every single one of the soldiers involved in desecrating the church killed themselves or met a horrible end! Sir Thomas Browne added that around a hundred brass inscriptions were taken away from gravestones and tombs during the civil war; the top of Miles Spencer's tomb was 'broken, splitt and depressed by blowes' and men used to 'trie their mony upon it'.

Taxation continued. On 11 April 1645, the city paid £500 as the first two months' rate towards New Model Army. Meat and beer were taxed heavily in the form of excise, and Norwich rose up against these levies. November 1646 saw anti-excise riots from the butchers, led by William Sheringham, James Sheringham, William Gaywood and John Phillips. 1646 had already been a difficult year, with the plague at Norwich and a flood in mid-November.

James Sheringham was one of the first apprehended. As soon as the butchers in the market place found out about it, they came 'furiously & tumultuosly [sic]' and rescued him 'violently'. The messengers were beaten and the clothes torn off their backs. The following Monday, a crowd of butchers gathered with clubs and staves and marched to the market place. The magistrates told them 'upon pain of death' they should return home; but Peter Watson, described as a 'poor butcher' and 'remarkable mutineer', answered 'A pox of God upon those that begun this worke,' and the crowd erupted. The butchers were going to break open the gates, but were persuaded out of it by some of the crowd.

They were still mutinous in December. Alderman Parmenter – whose job was to collect the excise money – wrote about it in a letter: 'As for our butchers they are still as abusive as ever, and none of them will pay a penny, but give reviling language to them when we send to take notice what they kill.' One of John Phillips's sons hit an excise officer on the head with 'the saw of a beast', and James Sheringham's wife took up a cleaver and threatened to open an officer's head if he came into her shop. Parmenter added in the letter that he was afraid the brewers were going to follow the butchers' lead.

Parliament appointed two men in each ward to enforce the observance of the Sabbath and stop all festivals. Norwich, fed up with being told what to do, hit back by electing Robert Holmes as sheriff in September 1646 – he was a known royalist.

By 1647, there was more unrest. Food was expensive – beef cost five shillings a stone. On 11 November Captain Blackwell, by order of the Parliament, took the lead off the Bishop's palace and chapel, defacing the chapel, and letting the buildings out to poor people for dwelling houses and tap-houses. On 1 December 1647, apprentices petitioned Mayor Utting to let them observe Christmas Day – Parliament had previously issued a decree that more or less cancelled Christmas. Utting agreed, and sealed his fate.

At the beginning of April 1648, a petition was sent to the mayor's court saying that the authorities were lax in their reforms. The petition was signed by around 150 people who complained that the old ceremonies and service books were still being used, there were still pictures in the churches, a crucifix on the cathedral gate and roof, and an image of Christ on the parish house of St George's Tombland. The mayor, John Utting, ignored the petition.

Sheriff Ashwell, Mr Ket and Thomas Barret rode to London to inform against Utting. On 22 April 1648, Parliament sent a messenger to dismiss Utting from office and bring him to London to answer the accusations; they also decreed that he should be replaced by the alderman Christopher Barret. They accused Utting of letting royalist clergy preach in churches, permitting festivities on Charles I's accession day and allowing Roger Mingay, a royalist, to be elected as alderman in March 1648.

Utting's friends raised a petition to keep him in Norwich. The crowd, remembering how Mayor Gostlin had been removed, turned ugly. They gathered in the market place on the Sunday and called out, 'We might thank Tom Baret, but before we do, we will make him a poor Tom Baret indeed.' They also threatened to hang Parliament's messenger and the sheriff upon the castle-hill, upon 'Gardiner's mare' (the gallows), and hamstring anybody who wanted to take Utting away.

A rumour spread that Utting would be taken secretly in the night. The crowd locked the city gates and took away the keys. They gathered in the market place – some of them with arms – and although Utting begged them to disperse and told them he would not be taken away in the night, even more people assembled the next day, with a watchword of 'For God and King Charles'. Christopher Bransby reminded the crowd that if they let Utting be carried away, they would have a governor put in as they had at King's Lynn, they would all be tried under martial law and 'then we had as good be free of Catton, as free of the city, for freemen would have no freedom at all in any choice'.

On Monday 24 April, the crowd went to the King's Head in the market place, where Parliament's messenger had stayed overnight. The rumour spread that Utting was to be taken, so the crowd rushed to seize the messenger – but Utting and several of the city justices kept him safe, and the terrified messenger was smuggled out of the city.

Then the crowd turned on the Puritan aldermen. They started by attacking the house of the informer Sheriff Ashwell, breaking his windows and raiding his house for arms, wine and food. Next it was the turn of the excise collector Alderman Parmenter – though he'd already sent on the taxes he'd gathered, so the crowd didn't manage to seize the money they were expecting. Then the crowd heard that the authorities had sent to the cavalry for help, so they marched on Committee House, where the county arms and armour were stored together with ninety-eight barrels of gunpowder. The gates to the building were secured by Samuel Cawthern, the keeper of the magazine, but a shot from inside the building killed a boy in the crowd. The crowd erupted and stormed the building.

The cavalry arrived: Captain Richard Sankey's troops plus twenty of Captain Stephen White's troops. The eighty soldiers were joined later that afternoon by Captain Griffith Lloyd's troops, and quelled resistance in the streets of the parishes of St Peter Mancroft and St Stephen's. A pamphlet printed in London 1648 comments wryly, 'some execution was done in the Lanes'.

But gunpowder had been spilled throughout Committee House. Some rioters swept gunpowder from the stairs, and one even took a hatful home. Given the fighting outside, it was hardly surprising that the gunpowder caught light. Ninety-eight barrels of gunpowder went up. The huge explosion destroyed the Committee House (now the site of the Bethel hospital). It also blew out the windows of St Peter Mancroft church. The mason Martin Morley received £55 for shoring up the tracery of the east window – even though he'd been one of the people implicated in the riot. St Stephen's church and neighbouring houses also lost a lot of glass. Special parish rates were levied to meet the cost of repairing the churches. The 1648 pamphlet says: 'The blow was so great, that it left not a glasse window standing in Chapley field house, and scarce any standing whole in all the Market place; besides that, it reved all the tyles of the houses adjacent, and ruined severall houses.'

Forty people were killed by the blast and 120 were injured; the pamphlet decribes it gleefully as, 'behold here armes and there legges of dead men scattered: every where some tokens of Gods Justice on these wretches and mercy to his poore people'. Another pamphlet claimed that the wind blew fire away from the soldiers towards the rioters; it was also raining so hard, the rioters couldn't use their flintlocks.

A letter from a parliamentarian notes that the blow 'wounded and killed a great many of the Inhabitants, the certain number not being yet known, nor many of them that were killed as yet found, or can be known; for many were torn in Pieces, and teared Limb from Limb, several Legs, Arms, &c. being found in the Streets, there are already missing and mortally wounded at least 120 Persons, besides as many more which received slight Wounds and Hurts' – but according to him no soldiers were hurt!

The city municipal records say that the Tuesday after the riot should be 'set apart and kept as a solemn day of thanksgiving for God's deliverance of this city from the rebellious company of people that did rise against them upon Monday last.' Two preachers, Carter and Collings, were asked to preach at the cathedral that day, each getting twenty shillings as a reward. The court also gave £200 to the soldiers 'for suppressinge the rebellious persons in this Citty', plus a further £50 'for repaire of losse of horses and armes and healinge of wounded men'. This money was to be 'borrowed out of the hospital chest' until the money was awarded by Parliament (or a rate levied!). The city also asked three of the six troops to stay until the unrest was completely over, and paid for the soldiers' quarters.

The day after the Great Blow, Utting rode to Parliament. He was confined to his house in Brandon from 19 May to 1 July, then fined, as was alderman John Tooly, who had represented Norwich in parliament in 1640. Utting was sent to the Fleet prison for six months and Tooly for three; Utting was fined £1,000 and Tooly £500, the money to be paid to the Norwich Assembly (though in 1650 they agreed to reduce Utting's fine to £200 and Tooly's to £400). Both were barred from office.

Then the investigations started. Nearly three hundred examinations survive. Christopher Barret wrote to Parliament in May 1648, warning them that there were 'men of rank' involved in the disturbances. It seemed that the riot was planned in taverns the night before, particularly in the White Lion. On Christmas Day 1648, 108 accused rioters were tried in Norwich Guildhall by Sergeant Keeble and Sergeant Earl. Twenty-six of them were fined £30, seven were imprisoned and two were whipped. Eight were hanged in the castle ditches on 2 January 1649, including the saddler Henry Goward (who was seen as the ringleader), Christopher Hill the brazier, Anthony Wilson the blacksmith, William True the dyer, Edward Gray the 'oatmeal-maker', labourers Thomas and John Bidwell, and Charles Emerson. At the same time Tirrel, an old woman, and 'an other woman' (Mistress Styles) were hanged as witches.

By January 1649, all those involved with the Great Blow had been removed or prohibited from office. A third of the common council was purged; and in June 1649 there was no guild day, for fear of a riot. Norwich's rebellion was over. But when Charles II was restored to the throne, Norwich, remembering the Great Blow, was one of the first to celebrate.

18

RALPH'S REBELLION

Norwich Castle dominates the city's skyline, even despite today's multi-storeyed buildings. It was originally a symbol of the Norman conqueror; it's said that when Norwich citizens couldn't pay the king's tax-collectors, William set them to work digging the castle ditches and building the castle mound. But its high profile also made it a target for rebellions. In later years, the castle became a prison and place of execution, and finally it became a museum, housing some of the county's greatest treasures.

The origins of the castle are unclear. The Elizabethan historian Alexander Neville said that the castle was originally built by 'Gurguntus, the son of Belinus, the twenty-fourth king of Britain from Brutus'; his successor Guthelinus continued the work and the castle of white stone was called 'Gaergunt'. Neville also claimed that Julius Caesar built the castle and, when his kinswoman Blanche married Thenatius, the castle was called Blanchfleur after her. Gurdon, another early historian, claimed that the first castle at Norwich may have been built by King Uffa in around 575 when he created the Kingdom of the East Angles.

The nineteenth-century antiquarian Walter Rye was convinced that the castle mound was raised in Saxon or Danish times, with a stockaded castle (possibly wooden), and the earthworks of the mound were taken from the end of the ridge along Ber Street. He also said that the ditch around the castle was a moat at one point – the mayor's court book in 1676 refers to a committee turning a drain into the common sewer 'which formerly passed into the Castle Dike' and in 1344 John Athill was granted a licence to build on a plot 'by the dyke of the castle'.

One thing was for sure: building a Norman castle here was symbolic, because Harold's brother had been the Earl of East Anglia. According to the Domesday Book, nearly a hundred houses were destroyed to make space for the castle and earthworks at Norwich. The castle was invested as a royal palace in 1075, held by a constable for the king, and was the only royal castle in Norfolk and Suffolk (two of the richest shires in the country, at the time) until the castle was built at Orford in 1165 – which shows how important the city was to the region.

It's possible that the orders to build the mound (or at least increase its size) came from William Fitz-Osbern, the Earl of Hereford, who was joint viceroy in England together with William the Conqueror's half-brother, Bishop Odo. Fitz-Osbern used Norwich as his eastern headquarters, but within four years he was killed in a battle in Flanders. His elder son inherited his Norman estates, and his younger son, Roger, inherited the earldom of Hereford and the English estates. One chronicler refers to Roger as 'a youth of hateful perfidy', and he was to play a large part in Norwich's rebellion against William the Conquerer.

The first constable of the castle was Ralph Guarder – sometimes referred to as Ralph of Wader – who was the Earl of Norfolk and Suffolk and also lord of Gael in Brittany. He wasn't particularly popular in England because he was the only English earl to fight on William's side at the Battle of Hastings – he'd fallen out with Harold, who had outlawed him, so Ralph led a group of Bretons on the Norman side. Ralph was born in Norfolk to an English father and a Breton mother. His father, also called Ralph, was the staller or master of the horse for King Edward.

Ralph's rebellion began with his marriage to Emma, the sister of the Earl of Hereford, because the marriage was in direct disobedience of the king's command. Although it isn't known why William was against the marriage, it's probable that he thought both Ralph and Roger were dangerous and he didn't want them joining forces.

Throughout 1074, Archbishop Lanfranc, the regent, sent Roger several letters rebuking him and reminding him that he should be loyal to his king. Eventually, exasperated by the young man's hot-headedness, Lanfranc excommunicated Roger, saying that he should submit to the king's mercy and make restitution to him and any other man Roger had wronged.

Roger remained obstinate and in 1075 he permitted Emma to marry Ralph. Worse, the marriage was celebrated very ostentatiously – which, as they didn't have the king's blessing, was equivalent to flaunting their bad behaviour. The wedding was held at Exning, in Cambridgeshire. Ralph's Breton friends attended, along with bishops and abbots (who should have had nothing to do with the excommunicate Earl of Hereford, let alone agreed to be his guest at the 'bride-ale'!) and huge amounts of beer and wine were drunk. The guests started to complain about William, and according to the *Anglo-Saxon Chronicle*, took advice about 'how they might drive their lord out of the kingdom'.

Roger was already set against William. Ralph was his new brother-in-law and bound to help him (and was also known to be treacherous, because he'd fought against Harold, his former king). Waltheof, the Earl of Northumberland, Northampton and Huntingdon, was also at the party. Waltheof had joined a Danish attack on York only three years after submitting to William after the Battle of Hastings, so Roger and Ralph saw him as a natural part of their plot – even though Waltheof had married William's niece, Judith and should have been firmly on William's side. Roger and Ralph's proposal was that they should drive William out of the country, then divide the country into three. One of them would rule as the king, and the other two would remain earls; each would have a third of the country.

The next morning, once Waltheof had sobered up (and possibly talked to Judith!), he thought better of it and confessed to Lanfranc. Lanfranc made him do penances for the church, then told Waltheof he had to go to Normandy and explain the situation to William. Waltheof went to France, laden with gifts, and asked William to forgive him. William appeared to do so, and kept Waltheof with him – under extremely close supervision.

Meanwhile, Ralph and Roger rebelled openly. Ralph asked his family in Brittany and Denmark to help him. English Bretons came to his aid, and King Swegen sent Ralph a fleet under the command of his son Cnut and Earl Hakon.

Lanfranc moved swiftly to crush the rebellion and called the rest of England to his aid. According to the chronicler Simeon of Jarrow, Wulfstan, the Bishop of Worcester joined forces with Angelwin, the abbot of Evesham, and they stopped Roger crossing over the Severn to join Ralph. Odo, who was the Bishop of Bayeux as well as being the King's brother, and Geoffrey, Bishop of Constance, went to battle against Ralph just outside Cambridge. Realising that his forces weren't strong enough to resist them, Ralph fled back to Norwich – and Lanfranc reported to William that Ralph and his army were fleeing, and the King's men were chasing him.

Roger was captured and imprisoned. Waltheof was also put in prison. Although Waltheof hadn't actually done anything rebellious and had told William everything he knew, William saw him as a danger to the country because he'd listened to traitors, particularly when Waltheof's old Danish comrades were in the vicinity. Not that they did much – according to the *Anglo-Saxon Chronicle*, the fleet of two hundred ships decided that it wasn't strong enough to fight William, so Cnut went to York and looted St Peter's Minster instead.

Ralph entrusted the castle and a garrison into Emma's hands and fled to Brittany and from there to Denmark, hoping for aid from the Danish side of his family. The bishops of Constance and Bayeux then laid siege to Norwich Castle.

Emma would have had good cause to throw her lot in with William. Her grandfather had been William's guardian, her father had been William's best friend, and her family were connected to the dukes of Normandy. But she must have loved Ralph very much, because she defended the castle for three months, even though there was no sign of help from her husband or the promised Danish and Breton ships.

When she was finally forced to surrender, William was so impressed by her bravery that he gave her forty days to leave the country forever and the people at Norwich were given terms rather than being mutilated or cast out. Emma then joined Ralph in Brittany and they lived quietly for the next twenty years. She accompanied Ralph when he went on the First Crusade in 1096. He died somewhere between Nicaea and Jerusalem, but it's not known what happened to Emma.

At the Midwinter Gemot or Parliament of 1075, Roger and Waltheof were brought to trial. Ralph was condemned in his absence. Roger was imprisoned for life, fined heavily and his lands confiscated. His followers were punished by having their eyes put out or their hands cut off, and some were banished.

Waltheof defended himself, his sentence was deferred and he was kept in prison in Winchester until the Pentecostal Gemot or Parliament of 1076. Again he argued his case, but he was beheaded on 31 May and subsequently became a martyr, with signs and wonders seen at his tomb in Crowland.

As for Norwich's punishment, the Domesday Book records that thirty-two burgesses fled the town and others were ruined by confiscation of their property. The yearly 'farm' (the lease of the revenues from tolls and court fines) that the burgesses had to pay to the King was tripled to £90. Following Christmas at Westminster, the King decided to punish all who had attended Ralph's wedding in Norwich. Some had their eyes put out, some were banished, and some had to forfeit all they had. The King also installed a garrison of three hundred men in the city. Despite the King's punishment of Ralph, his arms today form the lower part of the Norfolk County Council arms, and the ermine on the arms may be a reference to Brittany, as Ralph was lord of Gael.

The King made Roger Bigod the constable of the castle in 1075 and also made him the bailiff – he was to gather all the rent from the castle, city and earldom. Though the Bigods didn't always do what their kings expected. On William's death, Roger rebelled against his son William Rufus; though Norwich in turn threw him out of the city, because the citizens wanted peace. Roger's grandson (also named Roger) was one of the signatories to the Magna Carta, and the fourth Earl of Norfolk (also Roger) helped Simon de Montfort take control of the government from Henry III.

Nearly forty years after Emma's siege, when the hill was considered strong enough to hold a proper stone structure, Henry I had the castle built in stone. It was one of the largest Norman keeps in England, at ninety feet square and seventy feet high; the Normans called it 'Blanchfleur' as it was built from white Caen stone (imported simply because Norfolk didn't have a good source of building materials). Henry I spent Christmas there in 1122 and Henry II garrisoned the castle in 1156.

In 1345, the castle was handed to the County of Norfolk and became the county gaol and the official residence of the Sheriff of Norfolk. It was also the city's place of execution – Robert Kett was hanged from the castle walls in 1549, and Richard Ingham refused to speak in court in 1566 and was pressed to death in the castle, with great weights laid on him.

Though torture didn't play a huge part in the castle gaol. It's thought that the dungeons were used as a prison – though they're much shallower than most people think, only a few feet below the castle floors. Prisoners were set to work on treadmills or treadwheels. They ground corn to make flour until 1844, and then the system was modified to pump compressed air around the prison. Public executions were held on the twin gatehouses in the nineteenth century. The last public hanging was in 1867 (Hubbard Lingley) and the remainder were carried out inside the castle.

The castle was extensively remodelled in 1789 and resurfaced in 1837 by the architect Salvin with Bath sandstone and limestone, as the nearest equivalent to the white Caen stone. It remained a gaol until 1887, when the new prison was built at Mousehold Heath; from 1891 the buildings were used to house the museum.

In the twentieth century, when the site was excavated for the Castle Mall shopping centre, it became the only archaeological site in England where parrot bones were recovered. The castle itself was extensively refurbished in 2001 at a cost of £11.8 million to include interactive displays and show off parts of the castle that hadn't been on public display before, including Norman column bases and part of the well. Though it's good to see that the polar bear remains in residence, in the same place he's been ever since the castle first opened as a museum, over a hundred years ago.

19

RIOT IN THE CATHEDRAL

Norwich Cathedral is more than a thousand years old, a haven of peace and quiet – but its origins are rather stormier, because it was allegedly built as a penance for the sin of simony. Herbert de Losinga (meaning 'flatterer') apparently paid William II a colossal £1,900 to make him the Bishop of Thetford and £1,000 to make his father the abbot at Winchester. There are three paintings in an arch in the cathedral showing de Losinga handing over money, being absolved and building the new cathedral. He also said in his letters, 'I entered on mine office disgracefully, but by the help of God's grace I shall pass out of it with credit.'

However, some experts feel that the story is just a romance, as de Losinga was an incredibly busy and energetic bishop. After he got the Episcopal see moved from Thetford to Norwich in 1094, he created five dependent priories (including one at Yarmouth), founded a leper hospital in the north of the city (this became a branch library – which, at the time of writing, in early 2003, is under threat of closure) and built the Bishop's Palace and monastery. Work on the cathedral began in 1096 at the east end. The stone came from Northamptonshire and Normandy, and the rubble core included Roman bricks from Caister. De Losinga didn't live to see the completion of his dream, as he died in 1116 and the building wasn't finished until 1145.

But what a dream! Norwich Cathedral has the largest cloisters and the largest close of any English cathedral. It also has the second highest spire in England after Salisbury, at 315 feet – though it's not the original spire, which fell down in the hurricanes of January

1362, was rebuilt and then struck by lightning a hundred years later! The resulting fire turned the stone pink in the eastern end of the cathedral. Bishop Lyhart, trying to make sure that the cathedral wasn't at risk from fire again, covered the nave (which is one of the longest in the country) with a fire-resistant stone vault. The spire was rebuilt in 1480 by the next bishop, James Goldwell, and it became the site of a daring feat in July 1798, when a 13-year-old sailor-boy called Roberts from Yarmouth was given permission to go to the upper window of the spire. Not satisfied with the view, he climbed out of the window and up to the top of the spire, then walked round it twice. Although the weather cock is the size of a large dog – nearly three feet tall and three feet wide, weighing half a hundredweight – Roberts spun it round a few times, then climbed down again.

The cathedral has two more unique features. Firstly, there are 225 carved and coloured bosses jointing the ribs of the vaulting in the nave, and there are over a thousand of them in the entire cathedral. The bosses tell the story of God from the Creation to the Last Judgement, and Bishop James Goldwell put his signature – a gold well – on every boss in the presbytery. Secondly, the wooden bishop's throne at the top of the steps to the east of the altar has two pieces of stone beneath it which may be the remains of an eighth-century bishop's throne used at both North Elmham and Thetford.

But this was all nearly lost in 1272 during a three-day riot between the citizens and the monks. The riot was one of the worst ever seen in the city; it led to the whole city being excommunicated, and brought the King himself to Norwich to settle the dispute. Though who exactly was to blame is very much open to question.

Relationships between the cathedral and the city had been poor for years. There were arguments between them over rights of common land and boundaries, which were eventually settled by a fine in the King's court. The citizens had been unhappy for some time about the way homes had been destroyed to make way for the cathedral and the monks, and the Benedictine monk community didn't help matters by trying to control areas outside the cathedral precincts. The monks claimed that the city charter didn't cover Tombland, Holmstreet (Bishopgate) or Spitelond (an area within the precincts of St Paul's Hospital, next to Cowgate), whereas the citizens felt that their charter covered the whole city. There were also arguments about the proportion of tax paid by the monks and the citizens to the King, and the fact that the prior tried to collect taxes he was not entitled to.

Matters came to a head in June 1272 on the last day of the Trinity Fair. The citizens had erected a 'quintain' or area for lance practice in Tombland. They set a post in the ground and put a six-feet-long piece of wood on the top; at one end there was a board and at the other end there was a bag containing 100 lbs of sand. The idea was that the lanceman rode at speed towards the board, hitting it with his lance. If he was good, he hit the board so it swung round, but he'd ridden away before the sand could hit him (though breaking his lance was 'esteemed an honour', according to the eighteenth-century historian Blomefield). If he missed, it was a disgrace. And if he hit the board but wasn't quick enough, the sand would knock him off his horse.

Many citizens used the quintain, including Geoffrey Brun, Stephen le Blunt, Henry Godale, Robert Bonenfaunt, Hugh de Coventry and Walter Drake – high-ranking citizens and magistrates who were later accused of being the ringleaders of the riot and punished accordingly. Brun and le Blunt were clerics who were handed to the bishop for sentencing, Godale and Drake were hung, and Bonenfaunt and de Coventry fled.

During the lance practice, a quarrel broke out between the citizens and the servants of the priory over the broken parts of the spears – as this was technically the citizens' land, the priory servants were at fault here. The citizens, still resenting previous arguments with the priory, drove the priory servants back to the priory. During the affray, the priory drew first blood when William le Messer shot a bolt from inside the priory and killed Adam de Newenton, one of the citizens. The city coroners arrested two priory servants for murder after an inquest, and in revenge the prior excommunicated the citizens.

A siege followed – according to the *Roll of the Crown Pleas*, a record of the court proceedings of the time, the monks shot at citizens with crossbows and wounded many. They also hung shields over the walls and acted in a generally warlike manner. The citizens tried to maintain peace – they even sent friars and nuns to the Prior to represent them, then each party chose arbitrators and they came to an agreement which the citizens sealed with their common seal. But then Prior William de Brunham refused to seal the agreement with the cathedral chapter seal, so it was clear he had no intention of sticking to any agreement.

The following Sunday, the Prior brought three bargeloads of armed men from Yarmouth – Norwich's traditional rival at the time, although it's more likely that the men came from the priory at Yarmouth, which was a cell of the Norwich priory – and they marched through the city, beating drums and sounding trumpets as if they were at war. A group of priory servants came out that night with their Yarmouth reinforcements, killed and wounded several citizens, and robbed the city merchant Alfred Cutler of £20. Robert le Cotiller, presumably a relation as 'Cotiller' is the French equivalent of 'Cutler', was another indicted in the riot. Then the priory servants broke into Hugh de Bromholm's tavern and drank all they could – then drained the casks onto the floor to waste the rest. They also allegedly burned down three houses near Greyfriars.

The citizens wrote to the King to complain about the Prior's actions. The next day, on 9 August, they gathered in the market place at Tombland to bring justice to the monks for making 'an illegal castle' in the city. Pope Gregory's Bull claims that everyone in the city over the age of 12 was called up by the town crier and bell, though clearly that can't be proved now. Most sources say that around 120 people gathered in front of the priory gates. John of Oxnead and the monk Bartholomew de Cotton claim it was more like 32,000, though that is clearly an exaggeration.

The citizens burned down the Ethelbert gate to gain entrance to the priory. Then they burned the parish church of St Ethelbert and allegedly stole its books, ornaments and images. The next thing to catch fire was the bell-tower next to the church, which stood between the Ethelbert gate and the Erpingham gate. Who actually burned it down is less clear. Bartholomew Cotton claims that the bell tower was burned deliberately by the citizens, who had thrown fire from slings at the top of St George's church in Tombland. The *Liber de Antiquis Legibus* (the Corporation of London's 'Book of Ancient Laws', which chronicles various events in the country's history during the thirteenth century) gives the citizens' version of what happened and notes that the priory smiths, as they fled the scene, accidentally set fire to the bell-tower.

What happened next was a scene of great confusion, and the sequence of damage isn't known. As for the damage itself, that varies depending on the source consulted. According to the monks, everything was burned down. The Pope's Bull claims that the cathedral, belfry, dormitory, refectory, infirmary, treasury, sacristy, guest chamber and the whole placed was burned down 'except three or four buildings'. Holinshed takes it even further, claiming that 'nothing was preserved except one little chapel'. However, that is clearly an exaggeration as the cathedral is still standing, and its stonework was relatively unharmed. While there are small traces of fire in the southern part of the choir and its pillars, experts believe these may be due to a fire at the cathedral a hundred years before the riot. The *Liber de Antiquis Legibus* says that only the woodwork in the cathedral was burned, plus anything that could be burned outside the cathedral was 'reduced to ashes', although John Causton, one of the monks, saved the cellar of the infirmary and the vaults by 'quenching the fire with the drink in them'.

Cotton claims that 'many monks, some subdeacons and some clerks' were killed – though only thirteen people defending the priory were recorded being killed, and none of them were monks. The monks fled and some of the citizens plundered the cathedral of books, gold, silver and vestments. We don't know where the monks gathered together again but they did make a stand, the day after the fire, because the records state that the prior killed John Casmus by hitting him on the head with a falchion (a broad, curved sword). The

King's letters patent refer to 'conflagrations, homicides and losses . . . in the town' as well as in the priory, recognising that the monks had at least a share of the blame in the riot.

In the middle of August, Henry III sent Hugh Pecche, Geoffrey de Percy and Ralph de Bakepuz to the city to deal with the riot and ordered the sheriffs and burgesses of Norwich to help his men. Matthew Paris's chronicle claims the King 'was highly enraged at this crime, and exclaimed, "By the affection which is due to our Lord, I will go and see into this deed of wickedness in person, and I will repay them according to their demerits." '

In September, Henry III decided to come to Norwich himself – at Bury St Edmunds on 6 September, he sent letters patent to William Giffard, the Constable of Norwich, saying that he was coming to Norwich to punish the offenders. He also commanded the bailiffs of Colchester to detain anyone from Norwich who came into their district. On 14 September, he arrived in Norwich. According to Holinshed and Paris, when he saw the ruins around the cathedral, 'he could scarely refrain from shedding tears'. However, clearly he saw faults on both sides, as he placed the citizens under the wardenship of Hugh Pecche and Hervey de Stanhou, and the priory and its possessions under the wardenship of Robert de Waucham, Prior of Dunham.

Following the trial, around thirty citizens were dragged about the streets by horses to the gallows, where they were hanged and their bodies burned. Others were hanged, drawn and quartered, and the woman who was accused of setting fire to the gates was burned. Out of those indicted, twenty-three had either been city bailiffs in the previous fifteen years or were close family members – and according to Blomefield, one of them was the King's own bailiff when the city liberties were seized (and the city's liberties weren't restored until 1276). None of the bailiffs was executed or fled. Notably, three women feature in the list of those involved – Christian, wife of William le Gredere (fled), Agnes, wife to John Olive (hung, along with her husband), Agnes, wife of John Scot (hung).

Henry III died on 16 November and Edward I confirmed the

appointment of Pecche and Stanhou, then ordered the sheriff to summon a jury to investigate what had happened. The sources differ about who did the investigating. The *Liber de Antiquis Legibus* says that there was an inquisition of forty knights. Bartholomew Cotton claims there were forty-eight knights – and goes further to say that they were all bribed by the rich citizens of Norwich, which isn't very likely! The jury decided that the church was burned by accident by the priory smiths, the prior had tried to burn the whole city and set fire to it in three places and was guilty of murder and robbery. Prior de Burnham was taken into custody to be tried by the Bishop, who let him 'purge himself after the manner of ecclesiastics' – Burnham died soon afterwards, possibly from guilt or even from fury that he'd lost everything.

At the request of Roger de Skerning, the Bishop of Norwich, Pope Gregory excommunicated the whole city. The Pope singled out 'the magistrates or bailiffs' as 'more culpable in the . . . excesses and . . . the principal doers of the same'. This meant they should be 'strictly denounced and avoided by all men, and incapable of absolution'. Their bodies weren't allowed to be buried in any ecclesiastical cemetery, and if they'd already been buried they should be 'exhumed . . . and cast out far away from Christian sepulture'. They would also be deprived of any benefices or fees, and their heirs 'to the fourth generation' weren't allowed to be clerks or 'attain to any honour in any religious house' unless they had a special dispensation.

Clearly the Pope was expecting some kind of penance because if the excommunication lasted for four months, any citizen in 'that realm in the neighbourhood' who had 'dealings' with the city of Norwich would cause all their citizens to be excommunicated too! According to Blomefield, when the bells were rung at Eye, where the bull was announced, one of the bells fell down and shattered.

In 1275 the city had to pay the Prior 500 marks a year for six years. A mark was a monetary unit which only existed on paper; it was measured at two-thirds of £1, or 13s 4d, so this was a total of 3,000 marks or £2,000, the equivalent of a hefty £1.2 million today.

The city also had to give the priory a gold pyx weighing ten pounds and worth £100 (or £6,000 in today's money) and make new gates for the priory. The Bishop lifted the excommunication in December and the Pope gave Norwich a General Absolution in 1276.

Building resumed at the cathedral. The citizens built the Ethelbert Gate in 1307, as requested, and then new cloisters were built, though they weren't completed until 1450. This was partly because the Black Death killed much of the workforce in 1349–50, after which there was a seven-year gap until work could continue, and partly because the builders were needed to work on other projects.

And then there was more or less peace between the citizens and the priory – until the Civil War, as noted in chapter seventeen.

20

CITY HALL

In his series *The Buildings of England*, the architectural expert Nikolaus Pevsner described Norwich's City Hall as 'the foremost English public building between the wars'. Despite this commendation, people either love it or hate it! The building has also been described as 'a modernistic monstrosity' and when it was built it gained the nickname 'Marmalade Hall' because of its bright orange colour. The comedian Norman Long, appearing at Norwich Hippodrome, called it a marmalade factory (just as, the previous year, the Shakespeare Memorial Theatre at Stratford-upon-Avon had been referred to as a 'jam factory'). And in 1944 John Piper wrote an article claiming that 'fog is its friend', though perhaps it should be noted that most of the criticism came from people who didn't actually live in the city.

For hundreds of years the city had used the Guildhall as the seat of government, supported later by Victorian buildings, some of them ex-pubs. St Andrew's Hall worked effectively as the town hall, for public meetings and ceremonies, and a building made of corrugated iron (known locally as the 'Tin Hut') housed the police station. But when the scope of local government activities expanded in the early twentieth century and government officials complained of the rats infesting their workplaces (particularly when the rats died under the floorboards, causing an intolerable smell), the city realised that we needed new buildings to house the council offices.

In the late 1920s Norwich City Council bought land for the city offices and asked the advice of the Royal Institute of British Architects in 1928. The Institute suggested that the city should ask the leading architect, Robert Atkinson, to supervise the development. Atkinson was the Principal of the Architectural Association School of Architecture, and he was also responsible for designing the Barber Institute of Fine Arts in Birmingham, St Catherine's Church in East Acton, Warrington town hall, the power station at Croydon and the Regent Cinema in Brighton. The council asked Atkinson to prepare a layout and ground plan for the building. Atkinson went a stage further and produced detailed floor plans of the hall, including a design for a tower looking like a helter-skelter. His proposed designs were never used but the ground plans were retained as a condition of entry for a competition in 1931 to design the new City Hall, with Atkinson as the sole judge.

The 143 entries were all anonymous, merely numbered, with the names of the architects in sealed envelopes bearing the appropriate number. The winning entry was number 134, by Charles Holloway James and Stephen Rowland Pierce of Bedford Place, London, who also went on to design the county hall at Hertford around the same time (described as 'a bold mixture of influences: Georgian revival, Neo-Classical and Swedish Romantic styles') as well as Slough's town hall. The city applied to the Ministry of Health for a loan of £200,000 to build the offices. This was refused. Meanwhile, the Ratepayers' Association opposed the new buildings, pointing out that the economy was in recession and the money could be spent on better things.

A second public enquiry was held in 1934 and only two people opposed the scheme. The cost of the hall, market place, gardens of remembrance and the widening of the streets (Gentleman's Walk, St Peter's Street, Bethel Street and St Giles' Street) was estimated at £384,000, which works out at around £20 million in current prices. This time, the Ministry of Health granted the council a loan, and the council took out a thirty-year loan for £226,000 to start work on the hall.

At last, after four years of arguments since the design competition, building work finally started in 1936 by Sir Lindsay Parkinson's construction company. The foundation stone was laid by the Lord Mayor, Councillor Walter Riley, and Sir Ernest White on behalf of the architects. At the time, claims were made that the building was based on Stockholm Town Hall (though that's a myth), and Riley said that although the view from Stockholm Town Hall was one of churches, the view from Norwich would be 'a vista of breweries'.

The architects described themselves as 'interlopers pinching the best job for 500 years' and were sensitive to the city's needs. They insisted that the ancient Sir Garnet Wolsey pub should be retained in the market place, despite the original plans for it to be bulldozed. They also gave the city the original perspective drawing from their competition-winning plans – the drawing was six feet long!

The main part of the building was finished in 1938 and the Minister of Health had approved plans for the completion of the building, but then war broke out in 1939 and work was stopped. Lack of money meant that quite a few of the original ideas were dropped. For example, the three archways envisaged by the architects became three doorways, and an angel for the top of the tower (like those over the south doorway) was dropped. The building itself was only half completed, so the intended enclosed courtyard became an open car park. The west side wasn't built and the stub girders are still visible on the north side, though the police station section was extended on the south side in 1966.

Even so, the building boasts a pair of bronze lions by Alfred Hardiman, who also sculpted the three figures on the building symbolising Recreation, Wisdom and Education which overlook the car park, and the sculpture of *Earl Haig* on horseback in Whitehall. There are eighteen bronze plaques in the doors by James Woodward which celebrate medieval and modern industries in the city, including wine bottling, soda-water works, the building of the City Hall, the brewing industry, aeroplane building, making wire netting, the building of the Norman castle, the landing of the Vikings, the Black Death, the hanging of Robert Kett, chocolate making, the mustard industry, the cattle market, shoemaking and silk weaving.

City Hall has the longest continuous balcony in the country – 365 feet long, spanning three-quarters of the building – and the five main rooms at the front of the building have interconnecting doors that can be opened to make it a single reception room 365 feet long.

The Clock Tower was criticised at the time of construction, partly because of the cost and partly because the citizens feared it would dwarf the Guildhall. The tower is 185 feet high and, if you include the tip of the lightning conductor, that makes the tower 206 feet tall! The clock faces themselves are fourteen feet in diameter, made of copper sheet with gold leaf. The clock strikes every hour from 7 a.m. to 10 p.m., seven days a week, though it stopped in 1995 when engineers found the bell's support and striking mechanism were badly corroded. The clock started striking again in December 1997. The bell was founded by Gillett & Johnston in 1937–8 and is known as 'Great George', after King George VI. It weighs 2.8 tons and has a diameter of 65.5 inches. It is sounded by a clock hammer, is the largest and deepest-toned bell in East Anglia, and apparently can be heard as far away as Wymondham if the wind is in the right direction. When the bell was first struck, it was nicknamed 'death knelly' because of its deep sound.

The first inhabitant of the new offices was a stray black cat. She had kittens in May 1938 and the Lord Mayor, Charles Watling, adopted one and brought the rest back to his house while he found homes for them.

King George VI opened the building on Saturday 29 October 1938, at the culmination of the city's civic week, in front of the biggest gathering in the city's history. He said he was happy 'at being in the capital of my native county on so important a day in its history'. The City Hall clock chimed noon and then the royal party arrived to a fanfare of trumpets by the Royal Norfolk Veteran Association. The Lord Mayor received them on the steps and showed them the council chamber of the Guildhall; then the King went to the war memorial in the gardens of remembrance and laid a laurel wreath with Flanders poppies.

Lord Haw-Haw (William Joyce) said he had a special message

for the people of Norwich in one of his propaganda broadcasts: 'The people of Norwich have a new City Hall. It isn't paid for yet. But, never mind, the Luftwaffe will soon put paid to it.'

They didn't.

Norwich became one of the regional centres for the Festival of Britain in 1951. This was designed to be a celebration of the British people, the land of Britain and British achievements in order to raise spirits and shake off the horrors of World War Two. Princess Elizabeth opened the festival from the balcony of City Hall before going to Castle Museum to open the Colman Galleries.

But City Hall managed to court controversy even in the new millennium with the City of Light celebrations, which included laser shows projected from City Hall to the castle. In fairness to the council, the celebrations were free so maybe we shouldn't have expected anything too exciting: but the fifteen-minute laser show accompanied by classical music at 7 p.m. was not popular. One of the sponsors said in disappointment later, 'there was no action, no atmosphere and the lasers even missed the castle.' And at the midnight laser show, the laser operator missed his cue to the midnight countdown!

The laser company claimed that the announcer told the crowd to look in the wrong direction and people should have been looking at City Hall, not the castle, to see the display properly. The company took the view that the council underestimated the number of people coming to the event, so the spectators squashed on the edges of the market place didn't get the chance to see it properly. It also said that the friends and family of a council employee went into a restricted area, got in the way of the laser operator and blocked the first four seconds of the countdown.

City Hall redeemed itself at the Lord Mayor's procession in 2000, when special safety fireworks that had never been tried before in Britain were used. The fireworks could be used in any weather (just as well, given the dampness of the day) and debris from them turned to cold ash in the air, so they were safe to use near crowds. The display lasted for four minutes and at the finale, with massive explosions sending clouds of smoke and some ash across the Market Place, the crowds burst into applause.

Nowadays, the architecture of City Hall is simply not discussed and the initial controversy over the design has completely died down. But its next-door neighbour, the Forum, as the newest building in the city at the time of writing, in early 2003, has had plenty of comment on its design. As with City Hall seventy years ago, people either love it or hate it!

21

THE GUILDHALL

Henry IV granted Norwich its first Charter of Incorporation in 1404, which gave it full city status and the rights to elect a mayor, collect its own taxes, hold its own court of law and own property in common. Norwich was one of the first places to have this right and was one of the largest provincial cities in the country at the time.

To celebrate the charter, the city's rulers built the Guildhall to act as the headquarters for the city administration. It's the largest medieval city hall outside London and was built on the original site of a tollhouse dating back to Norman times, which was used to collect dues from the market traders. The present undercroft of the Guildhall actually belonged to the old tollhouse and it may be one of the earliest brick vaults in England, as the building work in the vault is cruder and the bricks larger than the other fourteenth-century vaults in the city, such as those of the Bridewell and the crypt at St Andrew's Hall.

The Guildhall was home to the monthly Sheriff's court (the county court, which dealt with land, property and debts) and a weekly Mayor's court which dealt with apprenticeships, trade regulations and bylaws. It also housed the Quarter Sessions and the yearly Court Leet, and was where prisoners were detained while they were awaiting trial. Space was also needed for tax collection, storing records and the city regalia, and for accounting. Scribes worked outside in little lead-covered booths and the citizens could pay them to write letters, accounts, deeds or records of legal transactions. A deed of arrangement from 14 February 1415 allowed the mayoral elections to take place at the Guildhall, too.

Work began on the building in 1407. Norwich citizens had to give money towards the building or work on it for nothing during the day, and only the skilled craftsmen were paid, at a rate of 6d a day. According to the historian Francis Blomefield, who had access to records which are now lost: 'in an assembly . . . John Daniel, Robert Brasier, and 22 more, were elected to . . . consult how to raise money to build the gild-hall . . . they had a warrant to press all carpenters, carters and workmen.'

The work went so well in 1407 that the arches for the prisons were finished by the master mason, John Marowe. The following year, Walter Daniel and Robert Dunston were elected to supervise the work. Again according to Blomefield: '24 persons were chosen to collect the aid or tax laid on every inhabitant in the city . . . each constable had a warrant to press workmen, citizens and foreigners to work at the Gild-hall every day from 5 o'clock in the morning to 8 at night.'

Clearly many people were pressed into service – as happened with many other projects in the fifteenth century, such as cleaning the river – as the second storey was built in 1408. The roof went on in 1409 and another tax and impress warrant was granted. The building was first used in 1412, when the vaults were used as a prison. Over the next forty or so years, further additions were made. Records show that the porch was built in 1423–4 and the windows were glazed in 1453. The chequered flintwork on the east gable was also put in place in 1453, and as it's an unusual motif for East Anglia it was possibly a pun on 'exchequer' to show that this was where the citizens paid their taxes.

The building was expensive – an account roll from 1411–13 lists costs of £104 7s 6d. Most of this money was spent on materials, and half of it was for lead alone. Some of the boarding outside was probably coloured, as the account roll refers to three pounds of 'blank plumb' (white lead), two pounds of red, four pounds of Spanish Brown and a pound of varnish, along with two gallons of oil.

By the end of the 1400s the building comprised of the dungeons in the undercroft and a 'free prison' on the ground floor – men and women were separated, but at least the prisoners didn't have to wear chains. The most dangerous prisoners were held in the undercroft, including the martyr Thomas Bilney (whose story is told in chapter eleven). On the upper floor, there were two halls for council proceedings, courtrooms and a guest chamber. The three courtrooms were used regularly by the Guildhall Court of Record (which replaced the old mayor's court) until 1972 and by the Magistrates' Court until the new Crown and County Courts were built on Bishopgate in the 1980s.

There was also a small chapel on the first floor which was used for chantries and for the prisoners, and a spiral staircase led straight from the chapel to the dungeons. A priest was appointed there in 1467 and the chapel was dedicated to St Barbara the Virgin, the patron saint of prisoners. St Barbara was martyred in 283 and her tale is recounted in *The Golden Legend* or *Legenda Aurea*, a book by the Dominican friar and Archbishop of Genoa, Jacopo de Voragine. The book gives an account of the Gospels, the life of Christ, episodes from the Old Testament and lives of the saints. Apparently, Barbara was shut up in a tower by her father Dioscorus 'so that no man should see her', because she was so beautiful. When she became a Christian, he handed her over to a judge who told him to kill her. Her father did so and was immediately killed by lightning.

The Guildhall didn't have a kitchen but, as it was close to the market place and to several inns, there would not have been any problem catering for feasts. The building was mainly heated by braziers, and records show that in 1540 the city had to buy charcoal for the council chamber.

Disaster struck in 1512 when part of the roof and two timber-and-tile towers collapsed, but the roof was reconstructed in 1534–7 by the mayor, Augustine Steward, at a cost exceeding £200. Most of the costs were born by the aldermen. During the reconstruction, the chapel of St Barbara had its windows coloured green to comply with religious reforms, and fragments of the stained glass were gathered into the three windows at the end of the Mayor's Court.

The whole place nearly fell down in 1635 when it was undermined by saltpetre-diggers. According to Blomefield, the diggers worked in the vault under the council chambers and the holes went to a depth three feet lower than the building's foundations. The diggers only stopped when some of the aldermen went to 'the council at London'. By the seventeenth century, the chapel was in such a state of disrepair that it was completely rebuilt and housed the new Sheriff's office. In 1697 a new prison was built on what is now the site of the old subscription library, and most of the prisoners were sent there (though it wasn't without disasters – there was a fire there in February 1773 which led to 'two felons' being suffocated). The Guildhall was then used as a cloth hall and a market for selling yarn, and part of the ground floor was used to store the city fire engines.

When the shire hall was burned down in the mid-eighteenth century, the county assizes were heard at the Guildhall instead, and the yarn hall was converted into a panelled courtroom. In Victorian times, the building was altered substantially – the porch and south range were rebuilt and the windows (except the one in the east gable) were replaced. The mayor, Henry Woodcock, paid for the clock turret and illuminated clock to be added in 1850, on condition that the false ceiling in the council chamber was removed to show the beauty of the old timber roof.

In 1908, tradition has it that there was a proposal to demolish the Guildhall, which was narrowly defeated by the mayor's casting vote! During the Second World War, a special false wall was built in the crypt to hide the civic regalia and the city's most valuable records. The regalia are now housed in the Castle Museum.

Although the city administration offices have moved behind the Guildhall to City Hall, the court has moved to Bishopgate and the tourist information office has moved to the Forum, the Guildhall still has a role to play in the twenty-first century. It's now the site of the first Caley's café – another Norwich name whose story is told in chapter twenty-four.

22

THE ASSEMBLY HOUSE

The Assembly House, on Theatre Street, is one of the most unusual buildings in the city. In his series *The Buildings of England*, the architectural expert Nikolaus Pevsner points out that the only other city of this size in England with an assembly house is Bath.

The original site of the house was the Chapel and Hospice of St Mary's in the Field, founded by John le Brun in 1248. It became a secular college in 1278 and the cloisters and crypt were built; the crypt is still part of the present-day cellar. Because the priests trained by the college were neither monks nor friars, it was well supported by the Norwich guilds. The wealth brought in by the guilds meant that its chapel (which, according to Jan King of the Norwich Society, was built of flint rather than stone) was actually bigger than the church of St Peter Mancroft, which is the biggest church in the city centre! Until the Guildhall was built, the great assemblies of the town were held there annually to choose the four bailiffs who governed the city. Jan King adds that there was an annual procession on the feast of Corpus Christi, starting with light bearers and then a procession of thirty-one guilds with their banners. They were followed by the sheriff, the mayor, the aldermen and then the crowd.

In 1548 the Dean of the College, Miles Spencer, surrendered the building to the Crown, and the King then gave him the site. Jan King observes that the Dean had such a reputation for being successful in business that people used to use the marble top of his tomb in the cathedral to test their money! The chapel was destroyed and the remaining building was converted into a townhouse named 'Chapply Field House'. Spencer bequeathed the house to his nephew William Yaxley in 1569, and Yaxley sold it to Sir Thomas Cornwallis, who built a new hall onto the house.

Cornwallis's son Charles sold the house to Henry Hobart in 1609. It was used occasionally for assemblies and was leased out to tenants in 1692. Jan King says that some of the conditions of the lease stipulated that the house should not be used for a tavern, and that the sale of all potable liquors (except vinegar) was forbidden!

In 1754, John Hobart leased the house to seven citizens and aldermen of Norwich for five hundred years at a cost of £1,800 plus an annual rent of £5. A deed of covenant was then signed to convert the building into a 'house for assemblies', which it remained until 1856.

The year after the deed of covenant, Thomas Ivory and Sir James Burroughs designed the new Chapel Field House and Assembly Rooms. They converted the existing building and intended to extend it. However, they ran out of money, so the wings of the house are not regular! The new rooms were opened on 22 and 24 July, 1755. According to the *Norfolk Tour* of 1808, when the Assembly House opened, it had a large ballroom (66 feet by 23 feet) and a small one (50 feet by 27 feet), with a 27-feet square tea room between them; the doors could be removed to give a suite of 143 feet, lit by ten branches holding 150 candles.

The yearly assembly on guild day, after the mayor's banquet in St Andrew's Hall, does not feature highly in the city records – they simply state that the assembly was held and 'the appearance of the ladies was brilliant'. More famously, there was a ball at the Assembly Rooms on 21 December 1805 to celebrate victory at the Battle of Trafalgar, which was attended by over four hundred people. The ladies sat down first for supper in the music room, followed by the men at the second sitting; part of the rooms were roped off to accommodate dancing to the musicians in the gallery, and the dancing continued until four in the morning.

Madame Tussaud exhibited her waxworks here during her travelling exhibition before it found its permanent home in the Strand in 1835. And Lizst played here in 1840 – to a very disapproving reception, with the reviewer from the *Norfolk Chronicle* listening in vain for 'one strain of pure and sustained melody'. Other famous entertainment included the great Shakespearean actress Fanny Kemble, who gave readings from *King John* and *Much Ado About Nothing* to wide acclaim.

In 1856, the Chapel Field estate was put up for sale at auction. When no offers were forthcoming, it was broken into lots (the Assembly Rooms and the west wing) and sold.

The west wing became a ballroom when Frank Noverre, a dancing teacher, bought it and built a 70-foot by 35-foot ballroom behind it. The Noverre Rooms, as they were then known, remained popular for dances and concerts (including two yearly concerts by the Philharmonic Society) until 1901, when Noverre's son sold it to the Norwich High School for Girls. The Noverre Rooms were then used as a gym until 1938, when they became a recreation centre for the YWCA. The rooms were finally converted to a cinema by the architect of City Hall, Stephen Rowland Pierce, in 1950.

The Assembly Rooms were sold to Benjamin Bond Cabell, a freemason. They became known as the 'Masonic Hall' until his death in 1876, when his cousin sold the rooms to the Girls' Public Day School Trust. The rooms were used as the Norwich High School for Girls – it's thought that Edith Cavell went there briefly – but when the school outgrew it and moved to new buildings in 1933, the building was put up for sale again. When there were no bidders, the Girls' Public Day School Trust considered trying to remove the Assembly House from the list of ancient monuments, so it could be demolished. Jan King records that the Norwich Society and the Norfolk and Norwich Archaeological Society held a joint meeting and passed a resolution in December 1935 to preserve it. The Assembly House then became a warehouse until the War Office requisitioned the building as a camouflage school. The rooms were discovered by the renowned theatrical designer and decorator Oliver Messel, who was in charge of the camouflage school, and he was shocked that such a beautiful building was being wasted as a warehouse.

In 1950, the shoemaker Henry Jesse Sexton bought the Assembly Rooms and the Noverre Rooms. He formed the H. J. Sexton Norwich Arts Trust, with the aim that the house could be enjoyed by the whole community. He also paid for the restorations in the same year by Stephen Rowland Pierce. Pierce said that he had to wage battle 'with decay, dry rot, beetles, neglect and blitz'. The house needed underpinning and the central beam in the ceiling was rotten at one end. But eventually the work was completed and, on 23 November 1950, the H. J. Sexton Norwich Arts Trust presented the Assembly House to the city.

On 12 April 1994, disaster struck when fire destroyed the main roof and damaged the house. The house was restored and opened again on 14 February 1997. And today, it fulfils the function Sexton intended; it's enjoyed by the whole community and is a meeting place for various groups. A quiet place, where you can sit and relax and hardly know you're in the city centre.

23

WHAT'S IN A NAME?

Medieval Norwich was a hive of industry – its market was one of the biggest in the country so it's unsurprising that many of the names of the streets are associated with various industries and trades. Different industries were centred in various parts of the city, and the names of the streets give a clue as to what happened where.

Charing Cross was originally known as Tonsoria – from medieval Latin, 'workshop where woollen cloth is shorn' – and then Sherershil, from the shearers themselves. The cross itself was removed in 1732, though in the eighteenth century the street name became 'Charing Cross' as part of the fashion for copying London street names.

Fishergate runs along the north bank of the River Wensum; the medieval fishing community and herring fleet was concentrated in the parish of St Edmund, and the fish was landed at St Edmund's Quay. There is no connection with Fishers Lane, which was originally Sloper's Lane, named after makers of 'slops' or outer clothes that were slipped on.

Mountergate Street began life as 'Inferior Conesford' (or Lower King Street) and in the mid-sixteenth century became St Faith's Lane, a corruption of St Vedast or St Vaast. In the 1880s it became Mountergate. The original form of mountergate was 'parmentergate', from tailors and robe-trimmers.

Pottergate celebrates an industry that had actually left Norwich by the thirteenth century. Earthenware remains have been found in Bedford Street, which was originally part of Pottergate Street until it took its name from a pub, the Bedford Arms, in the nineteenth century.

St John Maddermarket was named after the red dye got from the madder root. According to the eighteenth-century historian

John Kirkpatrick, madder was grown in Norwich, and there are references to 'Madelmarkette' as far back as the thirteenth century. The market was in the open space at the north end of St John's church in Pottergate; by the eighteenth century the area was known as St John's Street and then St John Maddermarket. Westlegate, which runs from All Saint's Green, refers to 'wastel' – bread made from fine white-flour.

Trading was also an important source of street names. The Haymarket originally encompassed Hay Hill, but the market was apparently moved to the castle ditches in the nineteenth century, and for a time the area was known as Old Hay Market.

Orford Hill was originally known as Swynemarket, when the swine market moved there in the thirteenth century from All Saints Green; then it became Hog Hill. By the nineteenth century it had become Orford Hill, commemorating George Walpole, third Earl of Orford (1730–91), who gave a great deal of money to contemporary civic improvement programmes. Orford also had a humorous side which gave him the nickname of the 'Mad Earl' – such as harnessing four deer to his coach, and they were chased to an inn yard by a pack of hounds. He bet a friend that he could drive a flock of geese to London faster than his friend could drive turkeys. He won the bet because the turkeys roosted every night whereas the geese didn't.

Rampant Horse Street sounds raunchy, but it actually refers to the city horse market. The street itself was originally known as 'Horsmarket'. The Rampant Horse Inn (sometimes known as the Ramping Horse) was built in the thirteenth century and took its name from the market; the street name changed in the eighteenth century and the pub closed down at the beginning of the twentieth century.

Timberhill was originally known as 'Durnedale', although the origins of the name are obscure – it could mean 'hidden dale'. It became the swine market briefly, and the name changed to Old Swine Market Hill at the end of the thirteenth century; then became a timber market – although the name 'Timbermarket Hill' (later shortened to Timberhill) didn't come in until the sixteenth century.

The market itself was in Tombland in Anglo-Saxon times, but

moved to its present location after the Norman Conquest. The area was known as Mancroft (meaning 'common enclosure' or 'common land') and was laid out in rows with set areas for different trades, and the name of the narrow streets or rows that once bordered the much smaller market place were taken from the trades carried out there. Over the years, these included:

- Medicines – apothecaries, leek sellers (which may have been herbs rather than vegetables), spicers
- Grain – barley sellers, malt sellers, oat sellers, wheat sellers
- Food – cheese sellers, fish sellers, meat sellers, poultry sellers, pudding sellers (which referred to sausages rather than sweets!), sheep sellers, 'sourbread' (leavened bread) sellers, white bread sellers ('wastel' bread)
- Shoes – cobblers, cordwainers (shoe-menders), souters (shoe-menders)
- Textiles – drapers, girdlers, glovers, hatters, linen drapers, 'omansete' workers (i.e. made sheets, either just big enough to cover one person or used a loom for one person rather than two), parmenters (leather workers – tailors and furriers), scudders (leather-dressers – apparently this is peculiar to Norwich and refers to dressing white leather), tanners, whittawers (leather-dressers), wool sellers, worsted sellers
- Other goods – ironmongers, needle-makers, rope-sellers, skeppers (basketmakers), tallow sellers, wood sellers

But what of streets where there were lots of different types of trade? For Norwich, this is London Street – first known as London Lane in the eighteenth century, which Kirkpatrick says came about because of the amount of traffic through it and the sheer variety of its shops. It was originally known as Hosyergate after the makers of stockings, became Cutler's Row in the fourteenth century after the cutlery trade, and then Latone Rowe after the latteners, who worked with an alloy of copper, zinc, lead and tin known as 'latten'.

For a city that once boasted a church for every week of the year, it's hardly surprising that so many of the streets are named after the church that stands on it, from St Andrew's Street through to St Saviour's Lane. The historian Kirkpatrick shows that some of the streets had earlier names which weren't connected with the religious life of the city at all.

All Saint's Green was originally known as Swynemarket; this became Old Swynemarket in the late thirteenth century when the swine market moved to Orford Hill, Timbermarket in the mid-fourteenth century, and finally became Allderhallen (All Saints) Green from the mid-sixteenth century; though it briefly became Winnalls Street in the eighteenth century from St Winwaloe's church (later known as St Catherine's church).

St Martin at Palace Lane was originally Horlane, from 'dirty lane' or the 'harstone' which marked the city boundary. It became known as Whores Lane in the eighteenth century, but that was simply from etymology because this area wasn't the red light district of the city!

Thorn Lane, named after St Michael at Thorn (which was destroyed in the Second World War), was originally known as Sandgate, probably because the road surface was sandy; by the seventeenth century it had become Thorn Lane.

St Peter's Street was originally Uvere Rowe or Overrowe, as it was the top row of the market. And St Stephen's Street was originally Needham Street, meaning 'poor homestead' or (according to Kirkpatrick) 'mansions of the cattle', as there was originally a large common pasture from St Stephen's Street to Harford Bridges. The street became St Stephen's Street in the seventeenth century. St Stephen's Plain was known as Tuns Corner from the Three Tunnes Inn in the seventeenth century, and in the early twentieth century was known locally as Bunting's Corner, until Bunting's Stores were destroyed in the Blitz.

St Crispin's Road sounds as if it should be named after a church but there isn't actually a St Crispin's in Norwich. Though there is a connection, as Norwich was once well known for the shoe trade, and St Crispin is the patron saint of shoemakers.

It's well known that Norwich once had a pub for every day of the year, so again it's unsurprising that many street names take their names from pubs. The Back of the Inns was originally known as Cockey Lane, named after the stream which passed along the west side over the castle. By the early eighteenth century, it was known as the Back of the Inns as it ran behind the Angel, Bear and King's Head Inns on Gentleman's Walk – inns which were famous in their day for politics, theatre and entertainment, displaying everything from pythons to elephants to a 'strange monstrous hairy child'.

But before they were named after inns and taverns, some of the streets were named after different features. Upper and Lower Goat Lane were originally known as Stonegate – though as the first reference to paving the city streets isn't recorded until the early fifteenth century, 'Stonegate' probably means 'the stony street'. By the late seventeenth century, the two lanes had taken their name from the sign of a pub.

Dove Street was originally Holdtor Lane or 'ditch tower' lane, as a stream ran through it in the eleventh century and there was a tower at the end nearest the market. It became Dove Street in the seventeenth century from the inn sign of the Dove.

Mariner's Lane was originally Hollegate, meaning 'street in the hollow', because the flowing off the ridge on Ber Street hollowed out the road. It became St John's Lane/Street in the sixteenth century, after the church of St John Sepulchre in Ber Street, then Mariner's Lane in the eighteenth century from the sign of Three Mariners' inn. Ten Bell Lane was also known as Hollegate because of the rain hollowing out the street from Pottergate to St Benedict's. By the mid-eighteenth century it was known as St Swithin's Street, then took its name from the Ten Bells, though some experts have suggested that the lane was so-called because you could hear ten different church bells ringing from it.

White Lion Street was originally known as Saddlegate, where saddles and tack were made – its name changed frequently to reflect the exact trade, so it became Bridlesmith's Row, then

Spurrier Row, then Lorimer's Row (from larrimers or 'harness strap makers'). It became Lion Lane in the late seventeenth century and White Lion Street in the nineteenth century, from the White Lion Inn.

Golden Dog Lane was originally known as Brent or 'burnt' Lane, as it led from the church of St Mary the Burnt – a church dating from a fire at the time of the Norman Conquest and which was demolished after the Dissolution. It took its new name from the Golden Dog pub in the seventeenth century.

Other streets which took their name from churches and then from pubs include Three King Lane in Pottergate – this was originally Bachouse Lane (and a bakery was actually excavated there in the 1970s), and became St Margaret's Lane in the fourteenth century. Five hundred years later, it took its name from the Three Kings pub. Rose Lane was originally called St Faith's Lane, from the lost church of St Vedast (a Flemish saint); by the seventeenth century its name echoed that of the Rose Tavern. Grapes Hill was originally known as St Giles' Hill, after the church. It was renamed after The Grapes pub, which marked the boundary of Heigham parish – and according to Kirkpatrick, had a leaden boundary mark on the wall showing St Ethelbert being flayed.

Princes Street was originally Hundegate; popular tradition says that the bishop's hounds were kept there, and the name still survives in the church of St Peter Hungate. It became Princes Street in the nineteenth century, from the Prince Inn.

Buildings other than pubs have influenced the street names. Agricultural Hall Plain is named after the Norfolk and Norwich Agricultural Hall, whose foundation stone was laid on 25 March 1882 by the Earl of Leicester. Contemporary reports claim that a court ruling was aimed at preventing it from being built, although they don't say why, and it was officially opened on 16 November 1882 by the Prince of Wales. Nowadays, the hall is part of Anglia Television.

Bethel Street was originally Newport Street, possibly named after the market-place. It became Committee Street, after the Committee House which was blown up in the riot of 1648 (whose story is told in chapter seventeen), then became Bethel Street or Bedlam Street after the Bethel hospital built by Mary Chapman in 1713 'for the habitation of poor lunatics, and not for natural born fools or idiots'. This was only the second mental hospital in the country and Chapman's ideas were way ahead of her time; she recognised the mentally ill as suffering from an illness rather than being criminals or a subject for humour, and didn't make a distinction between those who could afford to pay and those who couldn't. The Bethel hospital is the oldest psychiatric hospital in the country that is still used for its original purpose.

Bridewell Alley was originally known as St Andrew's Lane, as it runs by the side of St Andrew's churchyard. William Appleyard, the first mayor of Norwich, owned a house there which became a 'bridewell' or prison for vagabonds (named after the London prison near St Bride's Well) in 1585, and the seventeenth-century writer Celia Fiennes called the wall of Appleyard's house opposite the church 'the finest piece of flintwork in England'.

Duke Street was built in the 1820s and named after the Duke of Norfolk's palace, which stood there earlier. Most of the palace was pulled down in 1711 when the Duke had an argument with the Mayor; the rest of it was pulled down in the 1960s to build a car park, which has itself recently been demolished. Exchange Street was also built in the 1820s, from Gentleman's Walk to Lobster Lane, and was the first new street since Norman times. Its name came from the Corn Exchange, which was built in 1828 and demolished in 1964.

Elm Hill takes its name from elm trees that stood there – John Kirkpatrick notes that elm trees stood there in Henry VIII's reign, though the street was in such disrepair that it was nearly pulled down in the 1920s. It was saved by just one councillor's vote.

Willow Lane was named for a similar reason: according to Kirkpatrick, the name comes from the willow trees which grew near St Giles' churchyard.

As for New Mills Yard – only in Norwich could we have a 'new' that referred to buildings dating from the fifteenth century! The mills were known as 'new' to distinguish them from Appleyard's Mills.

School Lane was originally known as Cockey Lane after the water course running through it. It became Crouch Lane in the sixteenth century from the church of St Crouch or St Crucis, which was demolished by the mid-eighteenth century. The street name reverted back to Little Cockey Lane, then became Hole-in-the-Wall Lane by 1830 after a pub that stood there and housed the original meetings of the Norwich School artists.

The original quarters of the city – Wymer, *Ultra Aquam*, Mancroft and Conesford – also had their name commemorated in Norwich's streets. Westwick Street is named after the old quarter of Wymer (or Westwick); it became Letestere Rowe (or Dyer's Row) in the fourteenth century, then Westwick again. Heigham Gates used to stand at the end of Westwick Street – known as 'Hell Gates' because of the steepness of the slope down from Charing Cross, and also both for the slums surrounding it and because the next gate along, St Benedict's, was known as 'Heaven's Gate' as it was on the pilgrim path to Walsingham.

Coslany Street refers to the district of Coslany, which was in the quarter of the city called *Ultra Aquam* or 'Norwich Over the Water', as it lay on the other side of the river. The area was originally an island among river marshes, so Sandred and Lingström believe that the name Coslany means 'the course of a river in meadowland' or 'a stretch of river with plenty of reeds'. Mancroft, as we have already seen, comes from 'common enclosure' or 'common land' and became the market place; and finally Conesford, 'King's Ford', became King Street.

And of course the river has its own tribute in Wensum Street. The street was originally Vicus Cocorum or Cookerowe, as it was where the city's cooks lived; the name changed to Fye Bridge Streeet in the nineteenth century, then finally to Wensum Street.

Some of the more unusual street names in the city include Tombland; it's nothing to do with the burial grounds nearby as its name means 'open space' and it was actually the site of the old market. Life's Green, on the other hand, is the burial area around the cathedral! In the same area of the city we find Bishopgate; this was originally originally Holme Street (from 'water meadow') and is one of the oldest streets in the city, possibly even part of a Roman road. It was called Bishopgate in the seventeenth century, from the city gate by Bishop Bridge.

According to Kirkpatrick, Bank Plain was originally known as Motstowe, from 'meeting place', as it was probably the meeting place of the old Anglo-Saxon burgh. Gildencroft has actually retained its name, meaning 'guild brethren's croft', since the thirteenth century. Part of the area was known as the 'justing acre' (where jousting took place) and there was also an observation hill called 'Tothille' near there.

Muspole Street took its name of 'mouse pool' or 'moss pool' from the large pool or spring that once existed there. One end of the street was originally called Soutergate (from the cobblers and shoemakers who worked there), though this became corrupted to Southgate in the nineteenth century.

Ber Street takes it name from the Old English *beorg* or 'hill', as it runs along the top of a ridge; it was one of the first roads in the Saxon settlement and may also have been a Roman marching route to Caister St Edmunds. It was known in the nineteenth century as 'blood and guts street' as there were a lot of butcher's shops there. According to Kirkpatrick, the trade had always been carried out there; the mayor's court rolls from the Elizabethan period record that Ber Street was the only place within the walls of the city where cattle could be killed, and it was known as 'carnifices de Berstrete'.

Gentleman's Walk was the only paved street in Norwich in 1800. It was originally called Nether Rowe, as it was the lower row of the market place. It got its name, according to Kirkpatrick, because when the gentlemen of the county came into the city (for Saturday session times and market days), this was where they walked and talked.

Norwich has also honoured the names of leading citizens of the past in its street names. Bacon Road was named after Richard Mackenzie Bacon, editor and owner of the *Norwich Mercury*. He also set up the Norwich Triennial Music Festival (now the Norfolk and Norwich Festival) and died in Costessey in 1844. His son

Richard became the editor of the *Mercury* and helped to found the Jenny Lind hospital.

Bignold Road was named after Samuel, the son of Thomas Bignold who founded Norwich Union. Samuel Bignold was the secretary of the Fire and Life societies for nearly sixty years and was regarded as its second founder, after his father. He was also Mayor of Norwich four times, MP for Norwich from 1854–7 and instrumental in the setting up of the Norwich Public Library – he actually laid the foundation stone.

Blyth Road was named after Dr Ernest Egbert Blyth, who was the last mayor and first Lord Mayor of Norwich in 1910. Blyth was a Norwich-born lawyer who won several Law Society exam prizes, but his real love was education and he only had ten days off sick in his fifty-five years of service to the city. He was chairman of the governors of King Edward VI school, the City of Norwich School, the Blyth School (which was named after him), the East Anglian School for Blind and Deaf Children, the Norwich High School for Girls and the Notre Dame School for Girls. He was also a member of the Silver Road mission and spent his Christmas mornings giving presents to children in the yards of the poorest districts.

Davey Place was named after alderman Jonathan Davey, who claimed he was going to put a hole in the King's head. When he declared this in the council chambers, a police guard was put outside his door and the turnpike roads were patrolled, just in case he was going to try to kill George III. To twenty-first-century ears, this is ridiculous – but it wasn't quite as extreme as it sounds, because it happened not long after the French Revolution, and Norwich had a reputation for being a city of Jacobins. Davey was only posing as a revolutionary, as he actually meant the King's Head pub on Gentleman's Walk, which he bought a week after his declaration and then pulled down. The King's Head was given new premises at the end of the new alleyway he created between Gentleman's Walk and the castle ditches. The King's Head was the pub where Parson Woodforde used to stay, and the Irish giant O'Brien – a massive eight feet four inches tall – was exhibited there in 1797. Davey Place was the first pedestrian street cut in the city since the Middle Ages.

Hansard Lane was named after Luke Hansard, the printer born in Norwich in 1752. Hansard was a quick learner and worked hard. He helped his employer Stephen White in various businesses, including engraving, bookselling, stationery, painting and boatbuilding, and slept in the corner of the shop. Once Hansard had mastered his trade, he went to London to earn his fortune, and won the contract to print Cobbett's accounts of parliamentary debates. As parliamentary proceedings were under privilege at the time, Cobbett got a three-year prison sentence for his reports! But Hansard prospered and, from only having a guinea in his pocket when he left for London, died with an estate worth £80,000.

Opie Street was named after Amelia Opie, the novelist, who had a house near the castle. She was the daughter of Dr James Alderson and caused a huge scandal when she married the painter John Opie – not only was he from a lower class than Amelia, he was divorced because his first wife had run off with an army officer. John Opie was part of the artistic life of Norwich – he painted a portrait of John Crome – and encouraged Amelia to write. She wrote her first novel, *Father and Daughter*, in 1801 and Sir Walter Scott said he'd cried over it. She moved back in with her father after John's death in 1807. In 1825, after her father's death, she joined the Society of Friends (possibly because she was interested in becoming the second Mrs John Gurney – he'd been recently bereaved and he was a Quaker, though he eventually married his cousin's daughter) and spent most of her time travelling and doing good works before her death in Norwich in 1853. Opie Street was originally the red light area of the district; some historians claim it was called 'Evil Whore's Lane' and 'Devil's Steps'.

Ninham's Court was originally Masters Court, but was renamed after the artist who sketched it frequently. Henry Ninham was born in the city in 1793 and became a drawing master here by 1830; he spent his spare time making drawings of the ancient buildings of the city, though he originally worked as an heraldic painter and John Sell Cotman recognised his work on the repairs of a screen at Attleborough church. He gained a reputation for fine draughtsmanship and as a printer and engraver of etching plates.

Pigg Lane was originally Wateryng Lane; its name changed according to various people who owned property there, but finally was named after Henry Pigge, who was the Chief Constable of the area in 1514.

Rigby's Court was named after Dr Edward Rigby; his surgery and apothecary's shop were there. It was originally called Pit Lane, referring to an old refuse pit that was filled up and paved over in the eighteenth century. Rigby himself – as well as being John Crome's first employer – was renowned as an expert in gallstone removal and rose to fame with a treaty on urology. He was also responsible for introducing the idea of vaccination to the city and had his own smallpox hospital, as well as a licence to keep 'twelve lunaticks' in a house in Lakenham. He had twelve children – including quadruplets, who were born when he and his wife were already grandparents themselves, and the city council gave them an inscribed silver bread basket worth £25 in commemoration!

24

SUPER CALEY'S CHOCOLATE FACTORY

Albert Jarman Caley's name is synonymous with fine Norwich chocolate, but he was originally a chemist rather than a chocolatier. He was born in Windsor, on 29 October 1829. His parents owned a draper's shop there which is now part of the John Lewis Partnership, although it's still called Caley's. In 1857, Albert moved to Norwich and opened a chemist's shop in London Street. He started manufacturing mineral water in his cellar in 1863 and business boomed, so he expanded to Bedford Street in 1864.

Albert's son Edward joined the firm in 1878, and the business expanded even more. They knew they had to move but needed somewhere with a large supply of good water to manufacture tonic water, ginger beer, selzer, potash and lemonade. There were possible premises in Chapelfield, previously occupied by George Allen the glove-cloth weaver. If the water was there, it would be perfect.

The ground was chalk and clay; a well was dug to a depth of 100 feet, and an artesian bore was started. A further 209 feet down, the engineers found the supply the company was hoping for. The firm installed pumps and spent the next year pumping the water to clear the impurities. Finally, the water ran clear. But was it good enough? When the water was analysed, the results showed it was better quality than any other in the district, so Caley's built the factory over the two artesian wells. The first bottlings from the factory were sold in May 1880 – some of them were opened twenty-five years later and were still in good condition! The wells are still there and, although the water is no longer drinkable, it was used for cooling chocolate products as late as the 1990s.

As well as ginger beer – which was the firm's speciality –

Caley's produced medicated water for doctors and chemists. Working hours were long, from 8 a.m. to 7 p.m., six days a week, and the only days off were Sunday, Christmas Day and Good Friday; the staff worked on Bank Holidays, too. Caley didn't exempt himself from this, as he and Edward dealt with all the correspondence and management, with the help of just one day book clerk, one ledger clerk and one manager.

Working hours were even longer in the summer, with extra staff taken on to cope with the demand for Caley's waters. The day started at 4 a.m. and finished whenever the work was done, which could be as late as 10 or 11 p.m. However, Albert refused to let his staff work on Sundays (except for attending the steam boiler) and would even draw the taps of the ginger beer vats himself at five minutes to midnight on Saturday to make sure that no work was done on the sabbath.

Albert Caley was very religious – a member of the Plymouth Brethren – and as such felt responsible for his staff. Manufacturing mineral water kept his staff busy in the summer months but sales dropped in winter, so he needed to find something else to give them continuous employment. He decided to start manufacturing a chocolate drink in 1883, because chocolate could be sold during the winter. The only problem was that no one at the factory had ever made cocoa. They knew the theory but the practice was another matter! Luckily, the suppliers of the machines sent along an expert to show the workers how to make cocoa.

The first attempts at cocoa were introduced at the Norfolk and Norwich Fat Cattle Show in the drill hall at Chapelfield. There were three different varieties: a sweet powder called 'prepared' cocoa, an essence of plain cocoa, and a flavoured essence called 'cocoamel'. It was a success, and then someone suggested that Caley's should make eating chocolates. In 1886, the company experimented using a technique that could have come straight out of a home kitchen. They boiled the ingredients for the cream centre in a saucepan, beat it on a marble slab, then poured it through a kettle spout into a mould made by a cork in some starch. Once they'd cooled, the creams were covered by hand – by someone who had seen it done but had never actually tried covering chocolates.

The experiment was successful, and Caley hired Monsieur Olgard, who had once been a chocolatier to the French royal family. Olgard brought another change to working practices – he persuaded the company to employ women, though Caley still felt that boys should have precedence if they could do the work.

Albert retired in 1894, leaving the business in the hands of his son Edward and his nephews Frederick and Stuart. Caley's had been experimenting with different sorts of chocolate boxes, and this led to a new product development for the company. One of the menders of mineral-water boxes made artificial flowers as a hobby, and the management team was so impressed by them that they persuaded him to make fancy boxes for the chocolates in the form of a flower. This led to the production of boxes and, in 1898, the production of frills for chocolate boxes was expanded to the manufacture of Christmas crackers. By 1904 Caley's had 700 employees and agencies in Canada, South Africa, Australia and India. But, despite their overseas trade, they used local products where they could, including making Swiss-type chocolate from the milk from Garrett Taylor's herd of Red Poll cattle at Whitlingham.

Caley's also helped to encourage local talent. The painter Sir Alfred Munnings, before he became famous for his equestrian paintings, was an apprentice to a Norwich printer and he worked on many of the wrapper designs for Caley's chocolates in the early 1900s. One of his paintings from 1900 shows the Caley's stand at the Leipzig Sweet Fair. Although Munnings didn't sign the picture, he wrote about it in his autobiography and it was authenticated by Christie's – and it was later to cost its future owner a lot of money!

That future owner was John Mackintosh, who bought the firm of Caley's in July 1932. The factory at Chapelfield had been built at a time of high building costs, and the economic pressure in the 1930s meant that Caley's was suffering substantial losses. Rumours grew that there would soon be a change of ownership, and locals were relieved when that owner turned out to be Mackintosh, the 'toffee king'. Mackintosh's firm had a very similar history and growth pattern to Caley's, as it had started in a pastry shop in Halifax fifty years before. And the chairman of Mackintosh's, Sir Harold Mackintosh who was John Mackintosh's son, proved to be sensitive to local feelings when he said, 'As a youngster, Caley's chocolate was the first chocolate I became familiar with and liked.' He added that he hoped to employ more workers, not fewer, and the business at Halifax would be entirely separate. The *Eastern Evening News* spoke for many when it said 'the acquirement of one of our foremost local industries may be regarded with every satisfaction by the citizens generally'.

Then Lord Mackintosh heard that the Munnings picture of the Leipzig Sweet Fair was coming up for auction. He sent an agent to bid for it but, unknown to him, the company secretary of Mackintosh had also heard about it, thought that Lord Mackintosh would like it, and secretly sent an agent to bid for it. The agents bid against each other, so the painting ended up costing pounds instead of a few shillings!

Mackintosh retained the Caley's brand name. Caley's Marching Chocolate (known as 'Marcho') was given to the troops in the First World War as part of their rations, to help them 'fight fatigue' and give them strength. It gained the Royal Warrant in 1932 and was still part of army rations in the 1930s. At the coronation of George VI, one of the soldiers lining the procession to keep the crowds back gave a small boy the chocolate from his rations. The small boy never ate it, and when he read about the revival of the Caley's name in 1996 he sent the original bar to the company, explaining that he'd kept it all those years.

When the Norwich factory was hit by the Luftwaffe during the Baedeker Raids in April 1942, production of Marching Chocolate ceased. The factory didn't resume work until 1956, when it was opened by the Duchess of Kent. In the meantime, other companies' factories helped out with production. The mineral waters were used by the royal family and in the House of Commons; though that side of the business was sold to a local brewery after the war.

Mackintosh merged with Rowntree in 1969 and the company received the Queen's Award for Exports three times. By the late 1980s, 1,100 people were employed at the factory. Nestlé bought Rowntree-Mackintosh in 1988; over the years, lines produced by the Norwich factory included Diamond, Black Magic Block, Mintola, Weekend, Neapolitan, Extra Creamy Milk Chocolate, Quality Street, Berkeley Selection, Double 6, Good News, Yorkie, Rolo, Munchies, Golden Cup, Secret and Cabana (coconut) bar – plus, of course, Caley's Marching Chocolate. And when the wind blew in a certain direction, the city was filled with the mouthwatering scent of chocolate!

But then in the 1990s Nestlé announced that they needed to close one factory in the United Kingdom. They announced the closure of the Norwich factory and the loss of 900 jobs in 1994 and the Chapelfield factory finally closed in November 1996. Three former executives acquired the Caley's brand and reintroduced Caley's chocolate – including Marching Chocolate in 1998.

Roger King from Caley's says, 'British chocolate was different in the old days because no one in those days substituted any of the cocoa butter with cheaper vegetable fats – a practice used by many major UK producers today. We're still using the old recipe for Marching Chocolate, but it tastes better now – the chocolate of the early 1900s was much grittier because the particles were bigger. In the early 1900s Caley's employed a new confectioner whose remit was to "take the grit out of the chocolate and put it into the salesmen," – but the formulation's still the same, with 70 per cent cocoa solids.'

As for the factory itself: the chimney was demolished in 2002, and the site will become a new shopping development for the city.

25

THE IRREPLACEABLE J. J. COLMAN

When Jeremiah James Colman died in September 1898, the Mayor of Norwich said simply that he was 'a citizen whom they could not replace'. Mr W. H. Dakin added that J. J. Colman was 'a household word among all classes of the community' and 'one of the noblest sons of Norwich'. Not only was Colman the head of one of the largest businesses in the city, he'd also played an important part in civic life – he was Sheriff of Norwich in 1862–3 and mayor in 1867–8, a magistrate for both the city and the county, the chair of the Trustees of the Norwich Municipal Charities, the city's MP from 1874 to 1898, the Deputy Lieutenant for Norfolk, chairman of the board of governors for various schools, and an alderman of the city. And the mayor presented him with the honorary freedom of the city on Tuesday 7 March 1893.

As well as all this, he was a devoted husband and father of six and one of the founders of the *Eastern Evening News.* And he made an incredible difference to the life of the workers in his factories. He regarded himself as their friend and neighbour as well as his employer and is possibly the greatest philanthropist the city has ever known. The *Daily Chronicle* in London perhaps summed him up: 'a man whom, if you met him by chance, you would remember'. For Colman, anything was possible; he used to say, 'We don't use the word "can't" at Carrow.'

The story begins in 1830 when Jeremiah James Colman was born in Stoke Holy Cross. He grew up in a house opposite his great-uncle Jeremiah's mill, and his Nonconformist religious and philanthropic views were nurtured when he joined Norwich

Young Men's Improvement Society and attended St Mary's Baptist Chapel in Norwich.

At the age of 17, he joined the family business, J. & J. Colman. He became a partner in 1851 when his great-uncle died; three years later, his father died and J. J. Colman was left in sole charge of the business. He realised that most of the two hundred or so employees at the Stoke Holy Cross mills lived nearer Norwich and travelling caused them problems. The workers had to be up at 4.30 in the morning to be at the factory by 6.00 a.m., which meant that most of them didn't get home until 7.30 p.m. If the mill were nearer Norwich, it would improve their quality of life. So Colman had his employees' welfare at heart as well as a grasp of sound business principles when he bought land belonging to the railway at Carrow: the site was next to the railway line and the river Wensum, so it had good links to London and the coastal port of Yarmouth. The move from Stoke Holy Cross to Carrow started in 1854 and took eight years.

Though the manufacturing side of things wasn't without its problems; in 1852 the firm was in court on a charge of carrying on 'a new and offensive manufacture' – because a local schoolmaster complained of the smell when Colman's started making cattle cake from the fibres left over from starch production.

The mustard mill opened at Carrow in 1856 and Colman brought in a new way of doing things; before then, mustard powder simply went to grocers in wooden casks containing between nine pounds and a hundredweight. Colman introduced the idea of small decorated containers and bright yellow labels so that his product would be recognised on the shelves. The bull's head trademark was introduced in 1855 and was one of the first registered under the Trade Marks Act in 1875. When the mustard mill opened at Carrow, Colman opened a seven-storey tin workshop at the same time, and by the 1880s it produced twenty-five different sizes of container: something to suit everyone.

In 1866, Colman was appointed as the mustard maker to Queen Victoria. When he was asked to sum up the secret of his success and how he made a fortune out of such a humble thing as mustard, he replied, 'I make my money from the mustard that people throw away on the sides of their plate.' Nothing went to waste at the mill. The husks of the mustard seeds were crushed and the oil extracted from them. Then the fibre from the husks was made into cakes, which were sold as manure, and the oil was refined and used as a lubricant.

Royal warrants came thick and fast after Queen Victoria's. In 1867, Colman's were awarded a warrant by Napoleon III of France, another by the Prince of Wales in 1868, and another by Victor Emmanuel II of Italy in 1869. As well as royal warrants, Colman's products won awards; at the 1872 Moscow Exhibition, his mustard won one of the only two grand gold medals awarded, and in 1878 Colman was awarded the French Cross of the Legion of Honour for the excellence of his products.

Colman wanted everything made on site. So the works had a foundry, a sawmill, a printing shop, a factory for boxes, a paper mill, its own fleet of barges, its own fire brigade (set up in 1881 after a serious mustard-mill fire), its own post and telegraph office, and its own water supply (after an artesian well was sunk in 1859). And, in typical Colman fashion, the first long-distance phone call in the country was made from its counting house to London in 1878.

Starch was another important part of Colman's business. His father and great-uncle had experimented making starch from wheat, potatoes and chestnuts, but finally settled on rice. In 1851, Colman's won an award at the Crystal Palace exhibition for their rice starch; eight years later, the rice starch works opened at Carrow. Colman also patented a special starch to make linen and cotton inflammable. As well as starch, the company made laundry blue; in 1862, the laundry-blue mill was opened at Carrow. It was made from raw indigo (which tended to turn the skins of the workers blue, too!) but by 1872 they'd switched to using ultramarine, and sold the new product as 'Azure Blue'. It was used in the royal laundry and won a gold medal at the 1872 Moscow exhibition. Colman's starch also did well in the same exhibition, as it won the only other grand gold medal (the other one being for mustard, which Colman's naturally also won).

Flour was the other main product, and in 1861 Colman transferred the flour mills to Carrow from Stoke Holy Cross. Again, Colman's was innovative; it was one of the first companies to bag its own flour individually, rather than supplying large sacks to grocers and bakers. In 1864, Colman's branched out into the production of cornflour, which won the only grand silver medal at the 1872 Moscow exhibition.

During his forty-four years as president of the company, Colman saw the number of employees swell from two hundred to over three thousand. And he was an example to other manufacturers about how to treat his workforce. An article in *Commerce* magazine in 1893, called 'An East Anglian colony', said the Carrow employees were 'the most well-cared-for mass of operatives in the world'.

This is due in part to his wife; J. J. Colman married Caroline Cozens-Hardy, the daughter of a north Norfolk landowner, in September 1856. Before their marriage, he wrote to her, 'I hope we shan't lead an ideal selfish existence, for I am sure that it won't be a happy one if we do. Influence, position and wealth are not given for nothing, and we must try and use them as we would wish at the last we had done.'

Caroline was definitely a woman after his own heart; she was a devout Methodist and shared Colman's beliefs in self help, mutual aid and thrift. Neither of them were teetotallers but they both felt that drink was responsible for many social ills, so Colman bought out the landlords of six out of the nine pubs within a quarter of a mile of Carrow and closed the pubs! However, he did build a coffee house at Trowse to give his employees a recreational facility.

Unlike the Cadburys, Colman didn't build a model village for his workers, though he did build houses for them in Lakenham and Trowse. He believed that all families should have land for growing flowers and vegetables, and set aside some of his lands for allotments for the workers at Carrow.

He established clothing funds, provident funds and compulsory accident insurance for his workers; if they weren't insured against sickness in a 'friendly' scheme, they had to join the works scheme.

He also built a school at Carrow in 1857 and told all his employees that their children could go there and he would pay teachers. Parents paid a penny a week (a halfpenny for second and subsequent children) and the money went to provide prizes at the school. Colman had strong ideas about what the curriculum should involve: he wanted it to include reading, writing, spelling, maths, grammar, geography, history, drawing and scripture. Though he was very even-handed about it, and insisted that 'nothing that bears the stamp of sect, party or denomination will intrude'.

The school started with only twenty-three children. It moved to new purpose-built premises in Carrow Hill in 1864, and by 1870 it had 333 pupils. Caroline, being practical, added woodwork, domestic economy and Venetian ironwork to the curriculum; and Colman, with his love of horticulture, added gardening and beekeeping. Matthew Arnold – the eminent Victorian philosopher, poet and educationalist, who was also a school inspector – visited the school and was impressed with what he saw.

Colman continued to pay for the school until 1891. Then he applied for a government grant, and from that point the education of the 637 children in the school was free. Colman's interest in education extended outside the company, too; he helped to establish a technical school in Norwich, and was involved in adult education and night schools.

The employees were looked after as well as their children. Caroline Colman started the works kitchen in 1868, to give the workforce cheap food and drink. A hot meal with a quarter of a pound of meat, plus gravy and potatoes, cost just 3d. This covered the cost of the raw materials, and the company paid for the preparation and cooking costs.

Four years later, Colman's set up a self-help medical club and dispensary. The employees paid 1d a week and this meant that if their wives or children were ill, they had free medical attention. Colman's appointed a sick visitor, too, to investigate cases of special need. In 1874, a welfare officer visited the homes of the female workers, and Caroline said her job was 'to teach them to be better women and better wives as they grow up'. Caroline herself distributed parcels and blankets (and advice!) to needy families from the works kitchen every October.

Colman also employed the first industrial nurse in the country; 32-year-old Phillipa Flowerday trained for a year at the Norfolk and Norwich hospital, then took up her post at Colman's in 1878 at a salary of twenty-six shillings a week. In her role, she had to help the doctor each morning in the dispensary, then did forty-five home visits a week, taking supplies from the works kitchen to the sick in the afternoons. She also assisted the Colman's sick society and administered a clothing club. When she married Colman's head gardener in 1888, her post was taken over by Sister Quarry.

Colman's also set up a residential home with a matron for its female employees. An article from *Commerce* magazine in 1893 points out that the firm provided lodging for girls for a shilling a week, including washing. It also listed the other employee benefits at Colman's – a clothing club, a lending library, the dispensary, schools of cookery and technique, workmen's clubs, savings banks, refreshment rooms, reading rooms, playgrounds for the young, athletic grounds, and '101 other good and noble helps to the healthy bringing-up'.

The staff also had a day's paid holiday. Colman's instituted an annual tea party on Whit Tuesday, but in 1877 there were too many employees to sit down, so he gave them a day's paid holiday instead. The office staff had a day off in September after the annual mustard delivery. Another typical act of kindness was on the Prince of Wales's marriage in 1863 – Colman gave a dinner in the Corn Hall to the aged poor of the city, seating over a thousand guests whose average age was 73.

In 1896, he turned Colman's into a limited liability company – but again he was thinking of his employees first and included a clause to make the directors of the company support charitable institutions. In his will, Colman gave £2,000 for twenty years to help employees, ex-employees and widows in need. In 1899 the Carrow works pension fund was set up in his honour; all members got eight shillings a week, plus what they saved by investing a minimum of two pence a week at three per cent interest.

So Jeremiah James Colman was an excellent businessman, a pillar of the community and an enlightened employer; his obituary also refers to the 'unvarying kindness and courtesy' with which he treated his employees. It also refers to his quick mind – he could see 'all the sides of a project at once and [eliminate] unnecessary detail' – and his 'reputation for strict integrity'; farmers never bothered haggling with Colman about the price of corn because they knew he would be fair.

But what was he like as a person? He was a quiet giant – he was over six feet tall and, although politics was a large part of his life, he didn't like the showiness of politics or municipal life. He actually refused to lay foundation stones, saying, 'I could not with sufficient dignity declare the stone well and truly laid.' He didn't actually say much in Parliament – but he was very committed to the cause of the Liberal Party and vocal about what he thought was right. In 1890, after a notorious adultery case involving MP Charles Stewart Parnell – an advocate of Home Rule for Ireland – Colman wrote to Gladstone to complain about his behaviour.

Perhaps the most telling thing about Colman's political life is that he refused Gladstone permission to ask Queen Victoria to give him a baronetcy. He was a straightforward and honest man; and he knew all about hard work. Even in his sixties, he got up at four in the morning to tend his gardens, worked through until 7.30 p.m., then went through the firm's accounts in the evening. But despite his rigorous approach to work he was thoughtful and courteous in his dealings with others, qualities confirmed by his obituary.

Towards the end of his life, Colman knew great sadness. His wife Caroline died on 5 July 1895; two years later, his son Alan died, aged only 30. Colman bought the site for a new children's hospital in Alan's name and made a children's playground so that his name could live on. Colman never quite recovered from the double loss and became ill in June 1898. He was also depressed by the death of Gladstone, who had been a personal friend. Colman wasn't quite well enough to attend his daughter Florence's wedding in September. Sadly, the family suffered two deaths in September 1898 – firstly Colman's mother, on 15 September, and then Colman himself on 18 September. Colman was buried in the Rosary churchyard, the nonconformist cemetery off Rosary Road.

Perhaps the last word on Jeremiah James Colman should come from George White, when he proposed that the freedom of the city should be presented to Mr Colman. White described him as a man 'whose eminent public services to the city, unostentatious generosity and estimable private life had endeared him to his fellow citizens.'

Colman's is now part of Unilever Bestfoods UK, and the 250 employees at the works at Carrow still produce mustard and other condiments under the Colman's brand name, such as apple sauce, mint sauce and horseradish sauce. Dry food mixes and Colman's 'Sizzle and Stir' are also produced at Norwich, and Colman's are still coming up with innovative products – their latest is the Recipe Kits. And long may they continue!

26

SHOEMAKER TO THE WORLD

It's hard to believe that only eighty years ago, children had terrible problems with their feet – fallen arches, flat feet, and other ailments that needed surgical correction. But thanks to one Norwich firm's innovation, the way children's shoes were made changed for ever. And for the better.

Start-rite shoes is one of the big success stories of twentieth-century Norwich, with its innovative designs for children. Today, the company has over 600 employees, sells 1.5 million pairs of children's shoes a year and exports all over the world. But the innovation actually started over two hundred years before, with the founder of the original company, James Smith.

James Smith, born in 1762, was the first person to make and sell ready-made shoes – not only that, he moved away from the Saxon manufacturing methods (that is, working on the shoe inside out) which other shoemakers were still using as late as the nineteenth century. Smith opened a shop in the Upper Market Place in 1792 for his ready-made shoes. His view was that making shoes to measure for each person 'made men dilatory' and he said it was better to manufacture standard sizes and sell ready-made shoes from the shop. Clearly it worked, because in the *Norfolk Chronicle* in May 1803 James Smith sent his 'sincere thanks' to 'his friends and the Ladies of Norwich and Norfolk for the very liberal support he has experienced'. He reassured them that 'notwithstanding the much advanced price of Leather' he would continue to offer shoes 'at his usual low terms', adding that he could also supply 'Turner's incomparable Blanching Cakes'.

He was succeeded by his son, Charles, who died in 1820. The

trustees of the company kept the business going for Smith's grandson, Charles Winter, the son of William Winter and James Smith's daughter Mary Ann. Charles Winter took over in 1827 and brought in some innovations of his own. In 1840, he was the first shoemaker to use the Singer sewing machine to make shoes (which could sew an incredible 3,000 stitches a minute). In nineteenth-century shoemaking, garret-masters cut the shoe uppers (called clicking) and the 'bottom stuff' (i.e. soles, heels and lining). Women sewed the uppers by hand, then passed everything to men for lasting. In 1856, Charles Winter brought hand-sewing machines into the factory and the shop in the market to close the uppers. And business was booming, because in the 1860s Charles Winter employed between eight hundred and nine hundred workers in the factory.

Charles Winter was also very much part of city life – he was a magistrate in the city, the sheriff in 1846 (when J. J. Colman was the mayor) and became the mayor in 1851. However, he died in 1867 and left the business to his son, Charles Smith Winter – who died only two months after his father.

In 1868, James Southall took over. He was a London accountant who'd married Marianne Wells (James Smith's great-grand-daughter) in 1857, a year after his first wife's death, and moved to Norwich in 1860. He joined the family firm, learned the business inside out, and in 1868 the firm became known as Willis & Southall when John Willis bought shares. Willis also took part in city life, being a magistrate and an alderman; however, he turned down the chance to become mayor due to illness. After Willis's death, the firm became known as Southalls again.

During the First World War, Southalls made lots of machine-sewn hospital slippers which made up for the export losses, but after the war the company needed something to replace the sales lost when a lot of the old export markets started to produce their own shoes. James Southall believed that the future was in children's shoes. After his death in 1920, his son Frederick took over; but he in turn retired in 1926, leaving the company in the hands of his brother-in-law Bernard Hanly.

In 1921, the Start-rite brand name first appears in the company minutes. The retailer Quant & Son of Bury St Edmunds sold boots and shoes under the trade name Start-rite – boots and shoes which were actually made by Southalls. An indenture from 1921 grants Southalls the exclusive right to use the name Start-rite; they had to pay Quant & Son a royalty of 3d for each dozen pairs of Start-rite shoes sold, with a maximum payment of £500 per year.

The company decided to put more emphasis on the Start-rite brand. The medical experts of the time believed that most of the damage to children's feet was caused by badly fitting footwear. Southalls thought that the best way to prevent damage was to make shoes that fitted children properly in the first place. Children's feet weren't the same shape as adult's feet, so this was the first attempt by shoemakers to prevent damage to young feet.

For a start, Southalls made lasts in the shape of a child's foot, not a scaled-down version of an adult's foot. They made a shoe with a 'Thomas' heel; the heel was almost tick-shaped with the longer side of the tick on the inner side of the shoe and there was support inside the shoe for the child's arch and instep. The new heel stiffener therefore helped with balance and growth. Southalls also thought about fitting shoes to allow for the growth of a child's foot.

James Hanly, Bernard's son and the next chairman, continued the innovative approach to shoes. The company's advertising at the time summed it up very neatly: 'Children's feet have far to go.' In 1943 Hanly ordered a nationwide survey into foot ailments and the scientific measurement of children's feet. The survey began in Norwich in September 1943, when experts from Southalls visited four schools and measured and drew the feet of 106 children. By the end of 1943, they'd measured 450 children's feet; then the orthopaedic specialist Dr Sayle Creer took Start-rite's shoe designer William Peake to various hospitals so that he could see the kind of problems that children suffered, which then made them need surgical treatment. The designer then had a much greater understanding of the task ahead of him, but he was helped by Dr Creer, who became the orthopaedic adviser to Start-rite.

The results of the survey proved that children's shoes not only required an elongated heel, but also that they needed specially shaped shoes that would let their feet grow properly without being damaged. They needed more space in the toes, a wider waist and more space for the foot inside the shoe As a result, Start-rite developed a range of 120 fittings, including different widths and half sizes – a real innovation in the market at the time. They also developed the Inneraze shoe, which had a built-in wedge that stopped the child's foot rolling inwards and therefore becoming flat-footed; merely putting a wedge inside the shoe would be uncomfortable for the children. The Inneraze wedge was made of plastic, so that it wouldn't distort or wear, and because it was built into the shoe it didn't spoil their look.

But, of course, there was no point in selling good shoes if they weren't fitted properly. So William Peake started fitting courses for people selling shoes – and even today Start-rite trains anyone selling its shoes how to fit them properly, sending a thousand fitters a year through its training scheme.

1955 saw another innovation: the first (and only) Royal Warrant for children's shoes, awarded to Start-rite. The Queen asked them to fit the royal children for shoes, and gave Start-rite the Royal Warrant for fitting Prince Charles and Princess Anne, including gold kid dancing shoes for Anne, and brogues for Charles that had his Gordonstoun School number (89) marked on them in brass tacks. The warrant was withdrawn in 1989 and replaced by a new royal appointment to Prince Charles.

And although the company plans to move its offices in 2003, it will still remain within Norwich at Thorpe Business Park, with a new £3 million distribution centre and head office. Children's shoes still have far to go.

27

THE LAST TRAM

The end of the nineteenth century saw an exciting new development in Norwich – the building of the trams, though they were resisted by the cab-drivers and the council forbade them to carry any advertising. Construction work began on 22 June 1898 and the cars were built by Brush Electrical Engineering Company, seating twenty-six people outside and twenty-six people inside. When some of the tram bodies wore out in 1923, new cars were built by the English Electric Company, seating twenty-six people inside and twenty-nine outside.

Electric Tramway number 1 ran from St Catherine's Plain in Trowse through to Fye Bridge. Electric Tramway number 2 was the St Giles Gates network; its track needed to be renewed in 1933. Walter Macfarlane and Co from Glasgow built a shelter and timekeeper's office on this route at Orford Place in 1928, at a cost of £650. The St Giles network included the Unthank Road and Earlham Road routes, which converged into the route on Chapel Field North and Theatre Street, though trams on Theatre Street were outward-bound only, to avoid the parked vans which delivered early-morning supplies to the market. Electric Tramway number 3 was the City Road, Bracondale and Silver Road route.

The first trial was held on 19 April 1900. A large number of people gathered by the Sprowston terminal, opposite the Prince of Denmark pub, to witness the first run. Two tramcars sat outside the front of the station for the official trial at 3 p.m. The first people on board were Messrs E. Reeve & Bainbridge, who were the solicitors to the company, and Mr S. Mealing Mills. They were followed quickly by A. E. Collins, the city engineer; then J. W. London, the traffic manager; J. D. Smith, the power station manager; and finally the chief of the New General Transport Company, Mr A. E. Winslowe.

Car number 29 pulled out of the yard just after 3 p.m. and the electric tram caused a sensation. It travelled along Denmark Road, and had to ring a warning bell in Magdalen Street to part the crowds – one man left the barber's shop mid-shave to see the spectacle! The tram then went along the single rail from Fye Bridge to Tombland and stopped at the Royal Hotel.

Everyone judged the trial a success, so the service was formally opened to the public on 30 July 1900.

As with all new systems, there were teething problems, and the *Evening News* commented that after 'delays that seemed to promise going on to infinity', the trams were finally working. By half past nine in the morning, fourteen cars were out on the Earlham, Thorpe, Dereham and Magdalen routes. Apparently women stood looking out of their bedroom windows, wearing peignoirs and curling pins, mouths open at the sight.

The Earlham car had a full complement of 52 passengers and took 144 minutes to arrive at the city terminus – passengers could have walked the distance in half the time! The tram company blamed the passengers, saying that they didn't know how to use the trams properly. Instead of waiting at the official loops and getting onto the cars while they were still in motion, passengers hailed the trams to stop for them at any point along the route. On the first run, passengers demanded a stop at eight places between the city cemetery and Heigham Street, a walking distance of about five minutes!

Clearly the conductor needed a while to get used to the new system, and the paper commented wryly that the conductor 'had not yet found his sea legs'. The drivers found it difficult, too, once they were fully laden. On Guildhall Hill, contemporary reports noted that the driver didn't allow for the weight of fifty passengers when he put the brakes on, because the 'car plunged down the hill with a considerable way on her'.

On the whole, the attitude of the public was 'unstinted

admiration' for the trams. Though the transport difficulties seen today were clearly in evidence even back then; the local paper said that there weren't enough tram cars on the Dereham Road route and it needed more than one every ten minutes – more like one every three minutes.

But the trams didn't last for long. The first route to go was on 19 April 1925, when the Aylsham Road track was abandoned, and the trams were replaced by motor buses. City Road services were withdrawn in October 1933 and Trowse services in February 1934. The last of the trams stopped running on 10 December 1935 and the last trip was by all accounts a party.

The paper reported that the last tram ran on the Newmarket Road–Cavalry Barracks route, to be replaced by 'the latest means of transport, the motor omnibus'. The tram ran from Orford Place to Eaton and back. At ten past eleven, 500 people gathered and packed the tram at Orford Place, cheering and singing all the way. When they reached the Eaton terminus, they sang 'Auld Lang Syne' for the twelfth time, followed by 'Old Faithful', 'The Last Round Up' and 'Roll Along, Covered Wagon, Roll Along'. Although the people inside the tram were 'sedate', those sitting on the top sang all the way to the terminus.

On the way back to Orford Place, a trail of bicycles and cars followed the tram. There was a collection for the conductor and driver – Mr Hill, the driver, had been with the tram company for thirty-seven years – and the passengers sang 'For He's a Jolly Good Fellow' all the way from the last stop to the terminus.

The last man to buy a tram trick was Mr P. Y. Coles of the YMCA in St Giles, though this was disputed by W. Bell of Sprowston Road.

When they reached the terminus, the crowd sang 'Auld Lang Syne' for the thirty-sixth time, and then it was all over. By 1955, the only places where you could still see tramway track were at the former tramway depot in Silver Road and in Thorpe Station yard.

The local paper wondered if, in fifty years' time, people would be writing in to say that they'd ridden on the last tram, and now they'd ridden the first machine of the new air service through the city. Sadly, that was a flight of fancy. Although we have an international airport in Norwich, air travel through the city itself still isn't feasible. The bus system which replaced the trams is still with us, and has even been extended to park and ride systems from the edge of the city at Costessey, the airport and Postwick. Although questions have since been raised about whether a tram system would actually be more reliable and run on time – and, at the time of writing in early 2003, the bus drivers were about to go on strike . . .

28

TRIUMPH AND DISASTER

Even our football team lives up to the Norwich motto of 'do different' – Norwich City Football Club is the only football team ever to win a cup and be relegated in the same season!

The 1984/85 Division One league campaign started reasonably well, with draws against Liverpool and Coventry, an away defeat to Tottenham Hotspur and a home win against West Bromwich Albion. But then a fire broke out in the early hours of Thursday 25 October in the main stand, gutting it and destroying the boardroom, the dressing room and a lot of souvenirs. The stand had to be closed but City weren't cowed and the season continued. City managed to win at home against QPR that weekend, following up with wins against Sheffield Wednesday and Luton Town. By the end of the year, City had drawn six, lost seven and won nine.

There was a promising start to the Milk Cup. City were drawn to play Preston North End away on 25 September in the first leg of round two and cruised into a two-goal lead after strikes from John Deehan in ten minutes and from Steve Bruce after thirty-two minutes. Peter Houghton scored for Preston just before half time, but that didn't dent City's confidence; within seconds of the start of the second half, Dave Watson was on target with a header to make the score 3–1. But ten minutes before time, everything went badly wrong. Keeper Chris Woods crashed to the ground with a knee injury; he continued playing after being strapped up, but Preston took advantage of the situation and, five minutes from time, Paul Wilkins reduced the home team's arrears. And then, only seconds from time, Peter Houghton scored a second goal for Preston to make it 3–3.

The second leg at Carrow Road saw City in scintillating form. Asa Hartford grabbed the first goal thirty minutes into the first half, and this was followed by a goal from Louie Donowa just before half-time. Mick Channon continued the run with a goal three minutes into the second half, and Steve Bruce scored with a header thirteen minutes later. Two minutes after that, Geoff Twentyman managed a goal for Preston, but on seventy minutes Hartford scored his second, and Donowa obliged with a flying header just nine minutes from time. Preston bore no grudges at the 6–1 win as they gave Hartford a lift back home to the north-west – and even waited while he had a medical so that he could sign for City! Manager Ken Brown said he hoped this comprehensive victory would give the team confidence in the league.

In the next round, the home match against Aldershot was nearly the shock result of the Milk Cup. It was the first time Aldershot had ever made it to round three, and they held City to a goalless draw. Ken Brown freely admitted, 'We were awful,' and that the team couldn't play as badly as this again in the replay!

And he was right. Despite the fog, it was a great match. Gary Peters of Aldershot scored an own goal after fourteen minutes but City didn't need the help because Dale Gordon made three goals: John Deehan scored just six minutes later, Mick Channon after sixty-one minutes and Peter Mendham on eighty-nine minutes. Aldershot didn't give up and battled bravely, but it was a one-sided match. City were through to the next round by the convincing score of 4–0.

Round four saw City play against Notts County on 21 November 1984. After a drab first half Mick Channon headed his way into the record books seconds before half time, with his three-hundredth career goal in his fiftieth cup match. On seventy-three minutes, John Deehan headed a second City goal. Four minutes later, just seconds before he was due to be replaced, Louie Donowa scored City's third goal (following this, he was selected for the England under-21 side). The final score was 3–0, and City were well on their way.

January saw City involved in the FA Cup, and the third-round match away to Birmingham City ended in a nil–nil draw. The replay, after extra time, ended in a 1–1 draw, as did the second replay. Two days later, Steve Bruce scored to give City a win in the third replay. A week later, Louie Donowa scored in the first half to give City the lead in their fourth-round away match. But then, unfortunately, West Ham scored two goals in the second half to knock the Canaries out.

But January also saw continued success in the Milk Cup. Grimsby was the only non-First Division side left in the competition and City were handed an away match against them. Manager Ken Brown said, 'The only better draw we could have had would have been Grimsby at home – it will not be easy . . . but it does give us a great opportunity.' Grimsby were in the last eight for only the second time in their history; on a previous occasion, in 1980, they'd lost to Wolves, who went on to lift the cup. Was this an omen? Would City go on to win the cup?

The match was in doubt as the country was gripped by freezing weather – and Ken Brown paid tribute to the fans who'd trekked up to Grimsby to sing their hearts out for their team: 'Our supporters tonight were fabulous . . . [they] came through tricky conditions, some not knowing if the game was on or off. They stood there in their thousands.' And they were rewarded with a headed goal after twenty-eight minutes from John Deehan: City were through to the semi-finals.

In the league, January and February were disappointing. There was a New Year's Day defeat to Ipswich at Portman Road, a home win against Southampton, thanks to John Deehan, an away loss against Liverpool (a painful 4–0) and a home loss against Nottingham Forest. On a practical front, plans were in hand to rebuild the damaged stand.

In the Milk Cup, February brought a tie to set East Anglian pulses racing. City had been drawn against bitter local rivals Ipswich Town. But given the recent reverse in the league, the omens weren't good for the Canaries, and many in Norwich feared it would be a repeat of New Year's Day. In addition, City had had a bad run in the league, and hadn't scored more than one goal against any opponent in that competition since November. In the first leg at Portman Road, the worst fears of Norwich fans were confirmed after only six minutes, when Ipswich striker Mich D'Avray scored with a header. City just couldn't get their act together and, at half time, Ipswich were 1–0 up, just as they'd been on New Year's Day. And it stayed that way. Ken Brown's comment was, 'We didn't play at all in the first half but at least in the second we battled well enough to give us a chance in the return.' An Ipswich spokesman hit the nail on the head, saying that they were surprised City got away with just a 1–0 defeat. Was this the end of the cup run? There was a second leg to follow in March, but would City be able to get and keep a two-goal lead over Ipswich?

In Division One, City pulled themselves together in March – from trailing 2–0 away against Queens Park Rangers they fought back strongly to earn a 2–2 draw, thanks to goals from Mick Channon and John Deehan. A week later saw another 2–2 draw at home to Aston Villa, with all four goals coming in the second half: the City ones from Paul Haylock and Gary Rowell. Then it was a 3–1 loss at home to Sunderland, followed by a 2–1 home win over Coventry City, thanks to Mick Channon.

In between, there was the second leg of the Milk Cup. City were trailing 1–0 and would have to score at least twice to win. John Deehan netted after thirty-five minutes to bring City level with Ipswich on aggregate. Ipswich had a chance to equalise in the opening seconds of the second half, but Alan Sunderland shot wide. It was looking more and more like extra time – and then, just three minutes from the end, Steve Bruce scored with a header!

City were going to Wembley. And the supporters went mad with joy; they invaded the pitch and lifted the team shoulder-high in triumph. Stan Petersen, the Lord Mayor of Norwich, said he was arranging a reception for the players, win or lose – 'It will be our chance as a city to say thanks and well done to Ken Brown and his lads.'

In the run-up, Norwich contracted football fever. It was City's Norwich's third time at Wembley; they'd been in the League Cup final twice before: in 1973 against Tottenham Hotspur and in 1975 against Aston Villa and both times they'd lost 1–0. Both times, they'd been in the 'visitors' dressing room – this time, they hoped to be given the 'home' dressing room. And they were: would it be a good omen?

City insisted that their match gear should be made by local firms, so Wensum Clothing made the suits and the shoes came from Rombah Wallace in Hingham. Mascots and gifts came pouring in from fans, including a lucky green-and-yellow teddy bear mascot from Drayton First School, which John Deehan's daughter Emma attended. Would it bring her dad enough luck to beat another record? He'd scored in every single round of the competition; could he do it in the final too?

Then injury struck. Steve Bruce had an ankle injury and Asa Hartford had a calf injury from the match against Sunderland. Luckily, they were both fit enough to be part of the team.

So on Sunday 24 March 1985, Norwich met Sunderland at Wembley in the Silver Jubilee Milk Cup final. Match commentators paid tribute to the atmosphere and the lack of trouble between the fans. The match went down in history as the 'friendly final' as there was a real carnival air among the 100,000-strong crowd, and there was even a sixty-a-side match in the car park before the match between the rival supporters! This was Norwich City's first competitive match on a Sunday and their first live televised game – against the side that had played against them in their first floodlit match, in October 1956. Another record had been broken, too – Asa Hartford was the first player to appear in three League/Milk Cup finals for three different clubs!

But . . . it was against Sunderland. Sunderland, who'd played them in their last Division One match and beaten City *at home*, 3–1. Could the team pull it off?

The team, managed by Ken Brown, was Chris Woods, Paul Haylock, Dennis van Wijk, Steve Bruce, Peter Mendham, Dave

Watson, Mark Barham, Mick Channon, John Deehan, Asa Hartford and Louie Donowa. Between them, in league and cup matches that season, they'd already scored fifty-two goals – eighteen by John Deehan, nine by Louie Donowa, eight by Mick Channon and six by Peter Mendham. With their best goal-scorers on board, surely City could win?

Just nineteen seconds into the first half, Sunderland striker David Hodgson hit a shot just over the bar, scaring City. Peter Barham then shot wide, and Deehan's strike in the twenty-eighth minute strike was narrowly saved by Turner. The first half ended goalless. But the game came dramatically to life just a few seconds into the second half. On the goal line, John Deehan took the ball from Sunderland's David Corner, then passed to Channon. Sunderland defender Gordon Chisholm got the ball but knocked it to Asa Hartford, who shot from twelve yards – it skidded off Chisholm and left Sunderland keeper Turner helpless. Just fifty-four seconds into the second half, City had scored!

The tide turned three nail-biting minutes later, when City defender Van Wijk was adjudged to have handled the ball inside the penalty area. Clive Walker came up to take the penalty for Sunderland, and City's supporters held their breath . . . and heaved a sigh of relief as the ball clipped the outside of the post. Then City's confidence returned and Barham almost got a second goal. And finally, the whistle blew. Norwich City had won the Milk Cup! Captain Dave Watson lifted the trophy and held it towards the Norwich fans, who went wild. We'd done it.

After the match, manager Ken Brown said simply: 'We played quality football.' Asa Hartford was modest about his goal: 'I don't know if I can claim the goal because I don't think it was going in . . . if it hadn't hit the defender . . . but then again I might as well claim it because it's as sure as hell the other fellow won't want it!' Though match commentators said that Chisholm had no chance of getting out of the way of the ball, so the goal wasn't his fault.

On the Monday night, the team toured the city in an open-topped bus and were welcomed by Stan Petersen, the Lord Mayor.

Around thirty thousand people were there to cheer them on the ten-mile route, twelve thousand of them outside City Hall alone, heedless of the cold and rain. The police were delighted to report that the fans were all well behaved and 'no trouble at all' – Ken Brown described then as 'second to none'. Patients sat in wheelchairs outside the Norfolk and Norwich hospital and sang 'On The Ball, City.' A trail of cyclists followed the bus up Harvey Lane; a police cordon held up rush-hour traffic on Aylsham Road for the bus. The firemen at Sprowston station sounded their sirens as the bus went past, and even pets were there on the route, dressed in City colours (and in some cases barking along to 'we won the cup').

Lord Mayor Stan Peterson presented the team on the balcony of City Hall, to wild cheers. Gary Rowell sang 'H'away the lads' and Mick Channon sang a Benny Hill song, then said we'd win the FA Cup next year as it's 'too cold at this time of year!' At the reception, Asa Hartford said, 'This is better than anything I have ever known in my time at any club.' And Steve Bruce melted the hearts of all the mums in the crowd when he gave his medal to his 6-month-old son Alex.

It was a fabulous moment. Norwich City were the winners of the Milk Cup, and were guaranteed a place in Europe. But in the First Division, things turned rapidly sour. A 2–1 home win over Coventry, thanks to Mick Channon, saw March out in style. And then the nightmare began. A home draw against Sheffield Wednesday, then five defeats in a row – Arsenal, Ipswich, Watford, Luton and Leicester respectively. Dale Gordon, Louie Donowa and Robert Rosario halted the run of defeats with a 3–2 away win over Stoke City – but then the defeats began again.

And eight defeats out of nine games meant that City were threatened with relegation. A scraped goalless home draw against Newcastle followed by a 2–1 win at Chelsea on a waterlogged pitch made things look brighter; although City were still in the relegation zone, Coventry would have to win their last three games to send Norwich down. Their last match was against Everton, the Division One champions – they'd never do it, surely! City could breathe a sigh of relief.

But Coventry managed the triple challenge. And City went down to the second division (incidentally, taking Sunderland with us – though City finished top of Division Two at the end of the 1985/86 season and stayed in Division One until their promotion to the Premier League in 1992). City couldn't even enjoy their first time in Europe – after the Heysel stadium tragedy, all English clubs were banned from Europe.

City were down. But at the time of writing, in early 2003, Norwich City are fifth in Division One, with a home tie against Dagenham & Redbridge in the fourth round of the FA Cup (and odds of 66–1 of winning the cup!). Who knows?

29

THE ONE AND ONLY BILL EDRICH

Bill Edrich was simply a phenomenon – a tiny human dynamo, at only five feet six, who played his heart out both on and off the cricket field. He was mainly a batsman, but he could also bowl and was more than useful in the field. Between 1938 and 1955 he played for England in 39 tests and scored 2,440 runs with an average of 40, including six centuries. As if this wasn't enough, he also took 41 wickets and held 39 catches.

Edrich represented Norfolk at Minor County level but was best-known for his career at Middlesex, which he represented from 1937 to 1958 (captaining them from 1953–7) and played 571 first-class matches. In his first-class cricket career, he scored 36,965 runs with an average of 42.39 including 86 centuries (nine of them doubles) and made more than 2,000 runs per season in nine separate seasons. He also took 479 wickets (with a best performance of 7 for 48) and held 526 catches. In 1938, he was the sixth man ever to make 1,000 runs before 1 June, and he made them all at Lord's, with an average of over 84. So it was hardly surprising that *The Cricketer* believed that Edrich, along with Compton and Hutton, was one of the 'three discoveries of a generation'. He was 24 when the war started and 29 when it ended, and had he been able to play cricket in this time, the consensus is that he would have been in the same league as cricketing legend W. G. Grace.

Though there was more to Edrich than cricket. He could have had an equally illustrious career in a different sport, as he captained his school football team and played for both Norwich City and Tottenham Hotspur before the Second World War. During the war itself, as a squadron leader in the RAF, Edrich won the Distinguished Flying Cross for a daylight attack as a bomber pilot. So William James Edrich was a man who didn't lack courage. In fact, the cricketer Trevor Bailey said he could never remember him flinching, no matter how hard he was hit with bat or ball. Edrich even batted with a fractured cheekbone in 1954, when he was hit in the face by Northamptonshire's fast bowler Frank Tyson and spent a night in hospital before resuming his innings. He never once cheated in a match, and his integrity was respected throughout the cricketing world.

His courage and ability can't be doubted, but his judgement may be a different matter. Edrich fell in love often, and followed his heart instead of his head. His first marriage to Mary was when he was only 20 years old and still an apprentice at Lord's. His second marriage, to WAAF officer Marion, was a surprise to the family but lasted until after the war. He carried off his third bride, Jessy, from an unhappy marriage in 1948; but the marriage broke up four years later after he fell in love with a girl during his Australian tour. And then at a cocktail party he looked across a crowded room, saw Valerie and informed his cricketing partner Denis Compton that he'd seen the girl he was going to marry. Compton was sceptical, but Edrich made her his fourth wife. And then he fell in love with Valerie's friend Margot . . . and even that didn't last, because he met his fifth wife, Mary, when he was 67.

Bill Edrich was also a bit of a whirlwind, with a legendarily volcanic temper, and he partied with the best of them, which contributed to him losing his place in the England squad. He could drink all night – even though he couldn't hold his drink! – and then insisted on driving home. He played a mean (though always fair) game of cards and drove much too fast. But his contemporaries all agree that he was a truly charming man, a man who was perfectly happy if a young player bowled him out in a minor game because 'it must be good for the game'.

His story began on 26 March 1916 in Lingwood, just outside Norwich, when he was born into a cricketing family. His grandfather Harry learned to play cricket at Bracondale School, Norwich, and played regularly for Burlingham Cricket Club until he was struck down with polio in 1903. Edrich's father, Bill senior, also loved cricket and played for Lingwood, as did his brothers.

The Edrich phenomenon came to the fore in Bill's generation. Bill, his three brothers and his cousin played first-class cricket for five different counties between them, and he and his cousin John both had distinguished careers in Test cricket. Bill Edrich played for Middlesex, his cousin John for Surrey, his brothers Geoff and Eric for Lancashire, and his brother Brian for Kent and Glamorgan.

They started young, too. Edrich first remembered taking part in a game of cricket at the age of 3, running after the ball that his brother Eric had hit with a miniature bat. The nursemaid had to take him in to bed, kicking and screaming, and half a century later he said that he would never give up cricket, it would have to give him up first!

Edrich's father taught him to bat, with their wicket chalked on the kitchen door. When he went to Bracondale school in 1926, he was coached by Jack Nichols, who had played for Lancashire and Worcestershire. Nichols endeared himself to the schoolboys by bowling them a 'gooseberry' – a ball which, if hit square on the leg side, would land in the gooseberry bushes belonging to the headmaster. If you hit the ball that far you had to collect your own ball, and Nichols turned a blind eye to the boys picking gooseberries. Edrich often said that this was how he developed his famous hook, because he loved the succulent red dessert gooseberries and made sure he hit the ball into the bushes!

Edrich was academic, like his father, and was being groomed to become a teacher. But cricket was an important part of his school years – he got his school colours as a team member at the age of 13, and in 1930 he took all ten wickets at a match against Norwich High School for only 18 runs and 49 balls! He scored his first century against Diss Secondary School (then took 8 wickets for 20 runs). In another match in 1931, he scored 149 not out – the next best batting score was only 5!

Nichols was so impressed with his young protégé that he persuaded Michael Falcon, the head of Norfolk cricket club, to take a look at Edrich's skills. Falcon was equally impressed and put him into the Norfolk Colts, the junior side – though he was taken off again to give the others a chance, when he took four wickets for just one run in four overs!

In 1932, Falcon saw another fantastic performance by Edrich against the Norwich Wanderers, when he scored 77 out of the whole team's score of 162. Falcon decided that the 16-year-old was ready to represent his county, so he joined the Norfolk team at the match against the All India team. In eight overs, Edrich bowled three maidens and also took the leading batsman's wicket (Nazir Ali) for just 11 runs. The All India team was legendary and Bill was terrified that when he went into bat, he would be out for a duck. In the end, the whole team was out for just 49 runs – and Bill had made 20 of them. He was the only player in the team to make double figures. In the second innings, he was one of only four men to get double figures – and *Wisden* commented, 'Edrich, a schoolboy, batted in promising fashion.' So promising that, during the next four years, he scored nearly 2,000 runs for Norfolk.

In 1933, the Depression had hit the Edrichs' farm. Bill senior gained a post as a manager on a Yorkshire farm, and at first it seemed that Bill junior would have to leave the school and cricket he loved – but then the headmaster at Bracondale stepped in and let him stay on as a boarder.

At the end of 1933 Bill had to make a decision: should he work for his degree – probably at Cambridge – and become a teacher, or become a full-time cricketer? He chose the latter and his father was furious. They'd all made sacrifices to let him finish school, so why couldn't he do his degree first? Especially as he would have to serve a two-year apprenticeship to become a first-class cricketer, because he'd been born and lived in a minor county.

It seemed that Edrich had made the wrong decision when Northamptonshire, the nearest first-class team to Norfolk, rejected him. Michael Falcon, the head of the Norfolk cricket team, believed that he would be good enough to play for England but also knew it could be difficult to earn a living in cricket, so he tried to persuade him to join Norwich Union. When Edrich refused, insisting that he wanted to be a full-time cricketer, Falcon talked Middlesex into giving him a trial, telling them that he would be the next Patsy Hendren or Jack Hearne, Middlesex's greatest batsmen of the time.

Then disaster struck. Edrich damaged his hand – very badly – in a farming accident, a couple of days before the trial. His mother gave him emergency treatment and his father tried to persuade him to cancel the trial, but he refused to miss his chance. And even though his wound split open again during the trial and drenched his glove with blood, he simply pressed a handkerchief over it and carried on. Geoff Fenner, the coach, saw what was going on and realised he'd discovered someone extraordinary. He was in.

But his dreams were set back yet again. The secretary explained that because of a mistake in paperwork and his registration forms not reaching Middlesex until October 1934, he wouldn't qualify until October 1936. Edrich accepted it philosophically enough (and had been talent spotted in the meantime by Tottenham Hotspur) but eventually he qualified for Middlesex, and in his first year he made three centuries. The next year, he scored more than 2,000 runs for them and was picked to play for England in India in 1938.

His opening season for England was disastrous. In six innings, he scored only 67 runs, and in the following winter in South Africa he made only 21 runs in five innings. But the fifth test was a record-breaking match in many ways.

For a start, it was the longest match ever played, with forty-three hours sixteen minutes of playing time – it took ten days and even then rain stopped play! On eight consecutive days when cricket took place the stumps were drawn before time – seven times because of bad light and once because of rain. The match also saw the biggest aggregate of runs in any first-class match (1,981); England's highest fourth innings score in a first-class match (654 for 5); South African's highest innings total in Test cricket (530 in the first innings); the record partnership in England–South Africa Tests (280 for P. A. Gibb and Paynter); the slowest hundred scored for South Africa in Test cricket (103 in six hours four minutes by A. D. Nourse); the longest innings played by a South African in Test cricket (seven hours eighteen minutes by P. G. Van der Byl); a record number of fifties (16 by both teams), and the slowest Test century scored for England (P. A. Gibb in seven hours thirty-one minutes, at 15.96 runs per hour). A record number of balls were bowled (5,463) and each side scored more than 900 runs (970 for England and 1,011 for South Africa).

South Africa set England a task of scoring 696 to win. Edrich batted for seven hours and forty minutes to score 219, including 8 fours in his first 50 runs (24 fours in his innings). Even though the light rain smeared his glasses and made it hard for him to see on the seventh day of the Test, he battled on, and the whole crowd congratulated him when he made his first century.

At teatime on the tenth day, the match was abandoned. Although England only needed 42 more runs to win, the rain poured down. The English players were simply unable to stay until the next day; that night, they had to be on the 8.05 p.m. train from Durban so that they could catch the *Athlone Castle* on Friday, because the ship's sailing time couldn't be changed.

Despite failing in eight tests, Edrich kept his place in the England squad – then lost it in 1939 before being named Wisden's Cricketer of the Year in 1940. The war meant that his cricketing career had to go on hold, while he trained as a pilot. After the war, although he'd previously played professionally, Edrich decided to go back to being an amateur. He continued to play for Middlesex, and although he'd previously been an opening batsman, in 1939 Brown and Robertson had established themselves as an opening pair, so his batting position moved to number three.

He played just one Test match against India, and was a late choice for the Australian tour of 1946. Australia was a trial of his courage. The wicket was so bad in the first test in 1946, it took Bill a hundred and five minutes to score 16 runs and he was hit ten times by the bowlers. *Wisden's Almanack* described it as one of the most skilful batting displays they'd ever seen. In his second test he scored 71 and 119 and nearly staved off an innings defeat; he was 11 runs off his century in the third test and made 60 in the fifth test.

1947 was Edrich's best year, and it was also a golden year for Middlesex when they could draw crowds of 20,000 to watch a county fixture. He scored 3,359 runs including 12 centuries at an average of 80.43, breaking a forty-one-year record for an aggregate (and only being beaten by his partner Compton, with 3,861 runs and 18 centuries, with an average of 90.85 – together, they took the two top places in the national batting averages). His top score was 267 not out, against Northamptonshire. Had Edrich not strained his arm at the beginning of August, which meant he couldn't bowl, he might have equalled J. H. Parkes's record of 3,000 runs and 100 wickets, as he'd already taken 67 wickets (6 of them for only 28 runs against Gloucestershire). In the 1947 tests, Edrich made 552 runs against South Africa at an average of 110.40, which made him the top batsman in the series. His partnership with Compton produced amazing figures – 228 in 196 minutes at the Manchester test, and 370 at Lord's. In the Manchester test, he made 191 runs – his highest score in Test cricket, made in five hours twenty minutes and including 3 sixes and 22 fours – and took 8 wickets off 57 overs.

1950 was the beginning of the end. In the first test he scored 71, but failed in the second test, scoring 8 in both innings. He was dropped from the team – partly because of his performance, and partly because he'd had a riotous late-night party during the first test against the West Indies. Edrich believed that life was for living and let tomorrow take care of itself – possibly as a result of his experiences as a pilot in the war – and he was known to be colourful, headstrong and sometimes controversial, as well as thinking that good parties always went on until dawn.

His party piece included singing (though apparently his knowledge of song lyrics was better than his actual singing voice!) and conjuring tricks involving an egg (which once went spectacularly wrong, to the cost of the white tuxedo worn by a cricketing correspondent). This didn't sit easily with the selectors, who judged the team would be better off without him. Or maybe it was because he'd got so drunk when celebrating Godfrey Evans's maiden test century that a porter had to put him to bed. 'I apparently went to bed rather noisily,' Edrich later confessed. And the chairman of the selectors, Bob Wyatt, was in the next room. Wyatt was furious at what he saw as Edrich's disgraceful conduct, and hauled him up before a committee at Lord's, which asked him to withdraw his name from the list of potential players for the 1950 tour of Australian. Edrich refused. The quarrel escalated and Edrich wasn't selected for a Test match for another three years. The decision wasn't popular with cricket followers, who demanded to know why he'd been left out when others were playing who were nowhere near his standards.

In 1955, Edrich was out for a duck in his final innings at Adelaide – though at home in Norfolk things were a little more illustrious, when he hit a century in a match for a Norfolk eleven against an All Edrich eleven. He resigned from Middlesex in 1957 when his batting average dropped to 22.92 – despite scoring 1,000 runs in the season – and at the end of the next season he returned to captain Norfolk, scoring runs and taking wickets until 1972. His only regret was that he hadn't been able to captain Norfolk to the championship of the Minor Counties.

He died less than a month after his seventieth birthday, in an accident that shocked everyone – he'd had a reputation for being indestructible, and even late in life he'd been known to climb a twenty-foot marble pillar in the middle of the hotel, just to prove that he could still do it! But after the St George's Day lunch in 1986, he came home, told his wife Mary what a wonderful time he'd had, then went upstairs for a rest. At the top of the stairs, he missed his footing, fell all the way down again and hit his head. Sadly, he died on the way to hospital from a fracture at the base of his skull. Fittingly, his ashes were scattered at Lord's, and he became as one with the cricket ground he'd always loved.

30

AND FINALLY

As Norwich is a place where we 'do different' there are some stories that don't quite fit elsewhere . . .

So let's start with the saints. Mother Julian aside, Norwich has had two particular saints associated with it. The first is St Walstan. He was an eleventh-century farm labourer who gave away his food to those he thought needed it more than he did. The farmer's wife thought he was mad and wanted to get rid of him – who knew where his seditious ideas might lead? – but her husband refused, however hard she nagged him. And then she found Walstan cutting a thorny hedge in bare feet. Why? He'd given his shoes away to someone who needed them more.

But . . . he was unscathed, despite the fact that there were thorns all around him. The farmer's wife realised that he was under divine protection and asked for his forgiveness. She then asked if she and her husband could adopt him, but he refused: 'I am soon to die.' Apparently an angel had told him when. He arranged for his body to be placed on an old wagon harnessed to two young bullocks that could go wherever they liked, and he wanted to be buried exactly where they stopped. The bullocks rested at Costessey, where a spring gushed up, then came to rest at Bawburgh where another spring gushed up. The church was built over it and apparently the well has never run dry . . .

Norwich's other saint comes from a rather nastier story – the first accusation of ritual murder by the Jews in England. It all started when a 12-year-old apprentice skinner called William was found dead on Mousehold Health in 1144. His body was mutilated and the townsfolk believed that he'd been tortured by the Jews.

The *Anglo-Saxon Chronicle* says: 'The Jews of Norwich brought a Christian child before Easter and tortured him with all the torments that our Lord was tortured with; and on Good Friday they hanged him on a cross on account of our Lord, and then buried him. The *Life and Miracles of St William of Norwich*, written by the monk Thomas of Monmouth, goes further and claims that the Jews hung William on a tree in Thorpe Wood, then bribed the Sheriff of Norwich, John de Caineto, with 100 marks (£66) to cover up the murder. The forester Henry de Sprowston discovered the body and claimed the Jews were responsible. Crowds came to look at the body; William was finally buried on Easter Monday.

According to Monmouth (who wrote the account years after William's death), William's uncle Godwin was a priest; he had the body exhumed, and the gravediggers were terrified when the earth moved and was thrown out at their feet. Godwin recognised the body as that of his nephew, had it reburied and then denounced the Jews at the next diocese synod. He demanded that the Jews should be tested by trial by ordeal, either of fire or by water – the Jews refused and the Sheriff gave them sanctuary in the castle.

A visiting prior asked if he could take William's body back to his Sussex monastery; the monks declined, but exhumed William's body. There was no sign of corruption and when he was buried in the cathedral cemetery, miracles happened – a rose bush on his tomb flowered in the middle of winter and people were cured by prayer at his tomb.

The cult waned, but then Bishop Turbe succeeded Bishop Eborard. Eborard had never believed the tale but Turbe did. And when a local moneylender, Eleazar, was killed by Simon de Novers, a knight who owed him money, and the Jews asked King Stephen to call de Novers to account for his crime, Bishop Turbe flourished his trump card – William's death. King Stephen adjourned the case indefinitely; and the miracles began reoccurring at William's tomb. Monmouth lists 115 miracles (over half of which happened to people within a ten-mile radius of the city), including the curing of insanity, blindness, ulcers, abscesses – and even curing pigs and oxen! William's body was brought into the chapter house and then into the cathedral; gradually, the cult died out, and his shrine was finally removed by the Reformation.

*

Norwich has been called a city of pubs as well as a city of churches, and its pubs have quite a few tales to tell!

Take the Wild Man on Timberhill, which was named after Peter, the Wild Boy. Peter was discovered by George I, who was hunting in the Forest of Herenhausen, near Hamelin, when he came across the 14-year-old boy. The story goes that Peter had been suckled by a she-bear in the forest. The King brought him to England and sent him to school, but Peter couldn't speak and clearly didn't do well at his studies. The King gave him a pension, which was paid to Mr Thomas Fenns to keep the wild boy; but Peter broke away from his keeper and somehow made his way to Norwich. He was incarcerated in the Bridewell as a vagrant, but then in 1751 there was a fire at the Bridewell. Peter was rescued and returned to his keeper; he died in 1785, aged 73.

The Billy Bluelight on Hall Road was named after a rather more local hero: William Cullum, the hawker, showman and athlete. No one knows how he got his nickname of 'Billy Bluelight', but one theory is that it was the Victorian nickname for a Temperance worker or teetotaller, as Billy was completely abstemious. Another theory is that it's from the naval signal for 'friend'. Billy sold wild flowers, heather, matches and cough lozenges; but what he was famous for was racing against wherry boats – on foot. He used to race the *Jenny Lind* steam boat, the *Waterfly* and *Yarmouth Belle* from the Foundry Bridge at Norwich all the way to Yarmouth. He died in 1949 but his name and the legend live on.

The Mischief Tavern dated back to 1599 when it was a merchant's house. It used to be known as the Fyebridge Tavern; by 1810 it was known as the 'Man Laden with Mischief', in 1840 as the 'Man with a Load of Mischief', and by 1850 it had been shortened to simply the 'Mischief'. The name came from the pub sign, which was based on a Hogarth painting – a cartoon of a man with a careworn face, carrying his wife on his back (with gin in her hand), a monkey and a magpie (signifying mischief and strife) on either shoulder, and a chain on his neck fastened by a padlock labelled 'wedlock'. It's possible that the sign was copied by John Crome.

Rather older is the Maid's Head, which dates back to 1287. It was originally the bishop's palace belonging to Herbert de Losinga, the founder of Norwich Cathedral (whose story is told in chapter nineteen). It was first let to the lay brother Hugh Bigod. It then became the 'Molde Fish' or 'Murtle Fish' Tavern, and legend has it that Edward the Black Prince was entertained there in 1350. The name had changed to the 'Mayd's Hedde' by 1472 (when John Paston referred to it in a letter to Margaret); it's possible that there is a link between the two names because the skate fish was once known as an 'old maid' in Norfolk. The Maid's Head was also home to younger, more nubile women – in particular a show by Dr Graham, giving a lecture 'to Gentlemen, on the Propagation of the Human Species, and on the Arts of exalting and rendering permanent the Joys of the Marriage Bed.' He'd already caused a scandal with his lectures in London on 'the Female', which starred Emma Hart, who later became Lady Emma Hamilton, Nelson's lover. Rather less savoury was the Pig in Misery, which had a communal chamber pot in a corner of the bar!

As well as drinking places, the city taverns were places of entertainment. The White Swan (roughly on the site of the Millennium Plain) was home to the Norwich Company of Comedians and Charles Macklin played Macbeth there in 1747. It was also a cock-fighting centre.

The Church Stile in the market place (roughly north of St Peter Mancroft) exhibited a live rattlesnake in April 1801; the snake was apparently 45 years old, and nine feet long. As part of the exhibition, it was going to be fed 'a quadruped'. Ladies or gentlemen who wanted to see it were charged a shilling, and children and working people were charged 6d.

The Angel – also in the market place – was first referred to in the Mayor's Court Rolls of the fifteenth century. As well as the usual strolling players and exhibitors, the Angel had some more unusual exhibits. There was a pair of elephants shown in 1685. In 1693, 'dancing on the rope and vaulting' was promised by Daniel von Straven and his servants. And then in 1815, Monsieur du Pain was billed as 'immersing his feet in boiling lead'!

The Rampant Horse Inn had a 'learned pig' which could spell and count – Parson Woodforde paid a shilling to see it in 1785. What was claimed to be the only rhinoceros in Europe was exhibited in the city in 1816. Rather larger pachyderms jammed the streets in 1952 – a herd of elephants! The date was 1 April but it wasn't a joke. The elephants belonged to Chipperfield's circus, which was due to perform in Norwich. However, due to bad weather, the rest of the circus was trapped in Ipswich and the elephants were the only exhibits to reach the city.

Norwich also had its share of gamblers – for example, Sir Lambert Blackwell. The story most often told about him comes from his bet in 1810 that he could drive a horse and carriage into Bank of England Court (just off Queen Street) and turn it round without touching the walls. The court isn't exactly large. But Blackwell did it – and won his bet.

But, given the proliferation of hostelries in Norwich, perhaps our last Norwich tale should end in a pub: with the Resurrection Men. In 1815, the host of the Duke's Palace was asked if he would be prepared to let a stable to an apple-merchant. Ben the ostler thought that the apple-merchant was a crook, but the host was more trusting and agreed. One night, there was a banquet in the city and some of the gentlemen attending it stayed at the Duke's Palace. While he was waiting for his guests to return from the banquet, the landlord fell asleep – but Ben the ostler didn't. In the dead of night, he heard wheels . . . and it was the apple-merchant.

When the apple-merchant left, Ben went to the stable and opened the last sack. What he saw shocked him, so he called his master to come and see what the apple-merchant had left. The landlord took one look and sent Ben to fetch Robert Paraman, the head constable and governor of Norwich gaol. Paraman came to the Duke's Palace and inspected the sacks; what he saw made him post a constable there.

The next day, the rector of Hainford came to town to tell Paraman that his parishioners had seen something odd in the churchyard on the previous night. Paraman nodded sagely, took him to the Duke's Palace and showed him the apple-merchant's sacks. The rector identified the dead bodies in the sacks as three of his parishioners who had recently been buried . . .

Perhaps the 'resurrection men' heard that they'd been found out, because the apple-merchant never came back to collect his packages!